域 外 遊

OFF TO SEE THE WORLD

詩 文 詞 • 出 匣 子 集

Poems and Essays
Out Of Box Collection

劉 月 新

YUEXIN LIU

中 英 對 照　　繁 體 版

Chinese and English　　Traditional Chinese Edition

ISBN: 978-0-578-28576-4

獻 給

DEDICATION

我的祖母

My Grandmother Lanya Zhou

分類目錄 CHAPTER TABLE OF CONTENTS

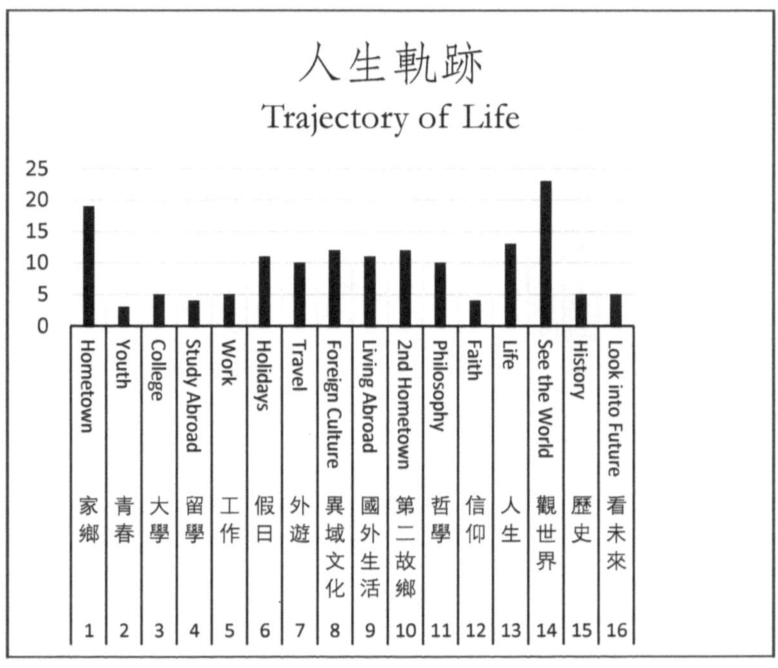
人生軌跡
Trajectory of Life
25
20
15
10
5
0
Hometown 家鄉 1
Youth 青春 2
College 大學 3
Study Abroad 留學 4
Work 工作 5
Holidays 假日 6
Travel 外遊 7
Foreign Culture 異域文化 8
Living Abroad 國外生活 9
2nd Hometown 第二故鄉 10
Philosophy 哲學 11
Faith 信仰 12
Life 人生 13
See the World 觀世界 14
History 歷史 15
Look into Future 看未來 16

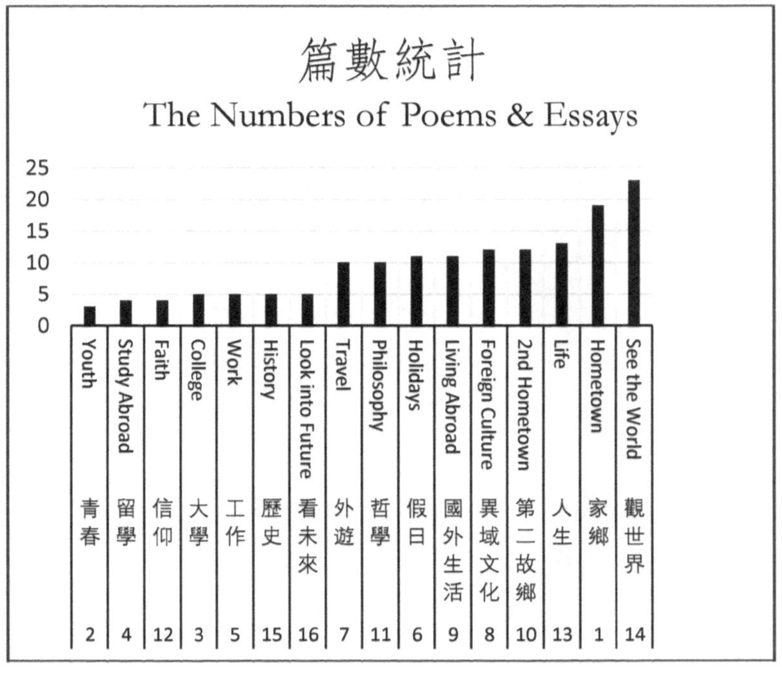
篇數統計
The Numbers of Poems & Essays
25
20
15
10
5
0
Youth 青春 2
Study Abroad 留學 4
Faith 信仰 12
College 大學 3
Work 工作 5
History 歷史 15
Look into Future 看未來 16
Travel 外遊 7
Philosophy 哲學 11
Holidays 假日 6
Living Abroad 國外生活 9
Foreign Culture 異域文化 8
2nd Hometown 第二故鄉 10
Life 人生 13
Hometown 家鄉 1
See the World 觀世界 14

ix

詳細目錄

DETAIL CONTENTS

域 外 遊　OFF TO SEE THE WORLD

2　青春　Youth　47

3　大學　College　57

4　留學　Study Abroad　69

5　工作　Work　81

6　假　日　Holidays　95

7　外　遊　Travel　119

8 異 域 文 化 Foreign Culture　155

11　哲　學　Philosophy　255

格式篇數

METRICAL FORMATS AND NUMBERS OF POEMS OR ESSAYS

格式	Metrical Format	篇　數 Number
七字詩	Seven-Character Poem	13
春聯	Spring Festival Couplet	10
短文	Essay	9
五字詩	Five-Character Poem	8
憶/夢/望江南	The Yangtze River South	5
千秋歲	Year of Thousand Autumns	5
四字詩	Four-Character Poem	4
水調歌頭	Prelude to the Water Melody	4
玉樓春	Spring of the Jade Tower	4
清平樂	Tunes of Purity and Peace	4
蔔算子	Divination Minor	3
滿江紅	Full Red River	3
采桑子	Mulberry Picking	3
鶯啼序	Prelude of Crowing Warbler	3
沁園春	Spring of Refreshing Garden	3
念奴嬌	Winsome Manner of Maid Niannu	3
木蘭香	Magnolia Fragrance	2
重樓疊月	Overlapping Towers and Stacking Moons	2
燕山亭	Pavilion of Mount Yan	2
行香子	Rite of Burning Incense	2
浣溪沙	Sand Beach of Silk Washing Stream	2
踏莎行	Treading the Sledge Path	2
江城子	Tune of Yangtze River City	2
一剪梅	Twig of Plum Blossom	2
永遇樂	Where it Forever Meets Glee	2
咨逍遙	Acclaiming the Leisure Manner	1
聲聲慢	Adagio of Tune by Tune	1
雨霖鈴	Bells Ringing in the Rain	1
定風波	Calming the Winds and Waves	1
賀新郎	Congratulating the Groom	1
蕙清風	Cool Breeze of Orchid	1
八聲甘州	Eight Tunes of Ganzhou	1
點絳唇	Embellishing the Crimson Lips	1

致 謝

　　這本書是我在工作和休閑的旅行途中寫的作品的匯集。偶爾我會把草稿發到微信上。我很感謝社交圈的很多朋友提供了之前的反饋，並鼓勵我繼續創作，堅持下去，最終發表。

　　在西雅圖，定期聚會的朋友們，每周都會與他們互動；登山隊的朋友們，在我們去迷人湖泊進行為期幾天的野營旅行之前，他們和我一起訓練了整整一年；來自本地區各大公司的同事們；當地的校友們；當然還有同屬第二故鄉、經常與之交談的西村人；他們從未停止挑戰我、幫助我、激勵我挖掘自己的想法。

　　在中國，我的父母、弟弟、妹妹、妹夫，以及下一代的孩子和年輕人，都對我的思考做出了直接和間接的貢獻。畢竟這一切都是來自生活的點點滴滴。

　　在網絡世界裏，一群來自 Freepik 的天才藝術家提供了很棒的圖形設計、水彩畫、圖案和幾何圖形。由於他們的慷慨，我得以完成封面的製作。

　　最後，我還要感謝我在西雅圖的家人對我的支持和愛。他們都讓我堅持下去，沒有他們這本書是不可能的。

劉月新

美國華盛頓州西雅圖

二〇二二年三月二十六日

ACKNOWLEDGEMENTS

This book is based on the collection of the pieces I wrote while traveling between home in Seattle and wherever the consulting projects or the leisure trips would bring me. Occasionally I would post the draft to the WeChat Moment. I am grateful for many friends of the social networking circle in providing the previous feedback and encouraging me to continue the work, persevere with it, and finally get to publish it.

In Seattle, the regular gathering friends, whom I interact with on a weekly basis, the hiking group friends, who trained together with me for a whole year before we made multi-day camping trip to the Enchanted Lakes, the colleagues from various big companies based in the area, the school alumni in the local region, and of course, the second hometown people I would have causal conversations with, all of whom never stopped challenging me, helping me and inspiring me to develop my ideas.

In China, my parents, my brothers, my sister, my brother in-law, and next generation of kids and young people, all made direct and indirect contributions to my thinking process. It is all about life after all.

In the cyberworld, a group of talented artists from Freepik offer great graphics designs, the watercolors, the patterns, and the geometrical shapes, which I could use to create the book cover.

Finally, I would also like to acknowledge with gratitude, the support and love of my family in Seattle. They all kept me going, and this book would not have been possible without them.

引 言

　　這是一本中英文現代詩文詞集。詩詞盡量以最流行的古典宋體格律填賦。短文試圖以簡潔而明快的風格寫成。集子提供了對世界和人生完全不同的視角和認知。

　　作品分 16 個類別，共 152 篇。從家鄉、青春、大學，到留學和工作，是關於人生的軌跡。假日、外遊、異域文化、國外生活和第二故鄉描述了不同國家的不同生活方式。然後是看待世界和人生的大視野，包括哲學、信仰、人生、觀世界、歷史和看未來。真正把所有這一切結合在一起的是出匣子式的思考主題。

　　我們已經習慣了每天所見所聞，總是被局限在一個下意識裏已經習慣的空間。這就是為什麼需要跳出框框去看外面的世界。當對新的世界已經熟悉時，我們清楚地發現，外面世界並沒有那麼大的不同。新世界本身也就變成了一個新匣子。我們需要不斷走出舒適區，找到新的舒適區，以一種螺旋上升的方式進行永無止境的叠代。

　　在中國長大和度過青春時期，讓我深深地繼承了中國哲學和東方思維方式。三十年的美國經歷為我提供了一種完全不同的看待世界和人生的方式。人生不是關於擁有一切。更多的是體驗一切。正是點點滴滴的人生本身，讓一切變得有意義。在人的某個階段，一切在突然間變得能自圓其說。由內而外。上下顛倒。螺旋上升。正是這種出匣子思維和敏銳的反思，貫穿著真正有意義的人生。本書試圖用中英文格律詩詞和短文的形式，以簡潔明了的語言來表達這所有的一切。

　　有些作品可能包含尖銳的個人觀點。美妙之處在於你不必認同。關鍵是思維過程本身，目的是激發新思想和新想法，是創造性思維和敏銳的反思。歸根結底，這個集子本身就是以出匣子思考為主題的作品集。

　　　　劉月新

　　美國華盛頓州西雅圖
　　二〇二二年三月二十日

域 外 遊　OFF TO SEE THE WORLD

INTRODUCTION

This is a collection of modern Chinese and English poems in the most popular classical Song style metrical formats, and short Chinese and English essays in the concise and sharp styles. The collection provides completely different perspectives on the world and life.

There are 16 categories with total 152 pieces in this collection of literacy works. From Hometown, Youth, College, to Study Abroad and Work, it is a trajectory of life. Holidays, Travel, Foreign Culture, Living Abroad and Second Hometown describe the different ways of life in different lands. Then comes the bird view on the world and life, Philosophy, Faith, Life, See the World, History and Look into Future. It is the Out-Of-Box thinking and sharp reflection that really pull all the things together.

Human beings are so used to what we see and hear every day. We are constantly confined to a domain that we are subconsciously accustomed to. That is why we need to see the outside world by going out of box. As we get comfortable with what we see and hear, it becomes clear that the outside world is not that different. The new world then becomes a box itself. We need to continuously get out of the comfort zone, find the new comfort zone and go through the iterations in a never-ending way.

Growing up and spending the youth in China allows me to be deeply inherited with Chinese philosophy and the Eastern way of thinking. Thirty years of American experience provide me a completely different way to look at the world and life. It is not about having it all. It is more about experiencing it all. It is life itself, bit by bit, drop by drop, that makes it all meaningful. At a certain stage of life, it all suddenly starts to make sense. Inside out, upside down. Spiral ascending. It is the Out-Of-Box thinking and sharp reflection that traverse a truly meaningful life. Attempts have been made here to express all these in a concise and articulate manner, in the forms of metrical poems and short essays, in both Chinese and English.

Some of the pieces may contain sharp personal opinions. The beauty is that you do not have to agree with me. And the essence is the thought process itself. The goal here is to inspire new thoughts and new ideas. It is the critical thinking and sharp reflection that I am aiming here. Ultimately this is an Out-Of-Box collection of literacy works after all.

域 外 遊　OFF TO SEE THE WORLD

域外遊序

　　樓上觀山，城頭觀雪，燈前觀月，舟中觀霞，月中觀佳麗，域外觀世界。所謂寰宇之大，必窮畢生心智而探之。方為無憾。

　　讀萬卷書，行萬裏路，嘗人間苦，閱世上事，納人指點，自己領悟。己走的路，別人走過。己做的事，他人做過。想的法子，人亦有過。所謂以鏡整衣，須從小至老站人肩膀。才能快捷。

　　海納百川，有容乃大，壁立千仞，無欲則剛。博古通今，融貫中西。見過了，到過了，做過了。站得高，看得清，遊刃有余。所謂大智若愚，方能為無為而無所不為。

　　八方九宮，四象五行，日月星辰，各循其律。金梭銀梭，上下求索。理想信念，青雲之誌。所謂盡吾誌而不能至者，可以無憂。

　　河出高山，一瀉汪洋。奇花初蕾，富麗皇皇。日新進取，盛氣希望。如俠似虎，冒險豪壯。所謂朝氣蓬勃，就象早晨八九點鐘的太陽。紅日東升，其道大光。

　　炎黃蚩尤，平常百姓，皇親國戚，朝代更叠。祖上陰德，比比皆是。成吉思汗，千萬後人，橫跨中西。先祖劉交，劉邦親弟，後也千萬。元子宋民，概中華人。同種同文，異種同習，都以華夏為族親。凡以色列人，人少不棄傳承，方能源遠流長，千年不息，立於世界民族之頂。

　　生本六十年代江南以西，自幼不比管仲樂毅。祖輩劉式、陳氏，享宋時五子登科、墨莊夫人盛名。明代劉伯溫亦五子後人。富不過三代，盛不會永在。家如此，國亦宜然，民族猶如是。只當長累厚積，方可經久不止。

三十年海外遊，八千裏來回走。每每默然回首，屢屢遠目星鬥。人生經歷積思想，賦詩填詞撰文章。常嘆長噓，漸寫下觀感心程。若堪造就裨益，勝得千古功名。

劉月新

美國華盛頓州西雅圖
二〇二二年二月十八日

PREFACE

Overlooking mountains from a towering floor, viewing snow from an elevated city wall, seeing the moon over a lighting shore, viewing the sunset with a wooden oar, watching beauties under the moonlight pour, observing the world from outside of territory door, these are all things I adore, I would only regret the things I don't do more, if I don't strive and pursue what I love to look for.

Reading ten thousand books, walking ten thousand miles, tasting the world sufferings, experiencing all sides and faces, receiving teachings from others, mastering the digestion with internalization. The intended path, other have gone. The planned undertaking, other have done. That witty idea, other have run. Learning from others is never late. Corrections with a mirror always aid.

Hundred rivers flow to the sea. Universe is only as big as leniency. Cliff stands solid thousand foot tall. More strength comes with less of wanting more. Knowing past goes with knowing present. Understanding Western comes with understanding Chinese inherent. Seen it. Been there. Done that. Standing high. Seeing clear. All things arrive with enough room to spare. It is as wise as it looks fool. It is as less intervention as many things you can explore.

Compass has eight directions. Sky has nine compartments. Change has four phases. Things have five elements. Sun, moon, star and universe, each has its own laws. Time goes by like a loom shuttle. From above to below, pursuing hard is vital. You only fail when you stop trying. Strong belief moves mountain. There is no regret when you keep doing.

The river coming from high mountain runs to the vast ocean. The splendid flower starts with the bud's burst motion. Constant renewing brings upon the prosperity. Steady drive sets the great expectation. Adventurous comes with marvelous. Audacity goes with creativity.

Youth is like the morning sun. The magnificence has just begun.

From Yellow Emperor to King Chiyou, from royal family to folks you never know, dynasties come and go. And there is royal descendant pole to pole. Genghis Khan has two hundred million offspring in Euro Asia. My far away ancestor, the young brother of the first Han emperor, who also has two hundred million descendants all over China. It does not matter if it's Yuan or Song, or whichever dynasty the people come from, they are all Chinese wherever they have gone, with the same culture and the same dawn, or from the same culture but different town. The Chinese nature is always real, just like the Jews from Israel. They always keep their heritage, which is why they are still strong in thousands of years of age.

From the south of Yangtze River, born in the 60s of the culture fever, never have I compared myself with Guan Zhong and Yue Yi of ancient Chinese sage master. Only lately from family tree, I came to know my ancestry. The chancellor of the first Emperor of Ming Dynasty, Bowen Liu, was in fact the offspring of the prominent 5-son Song officials of the same Liu family. Wealth does not pass three generations and prosperity is always in fluctuations. This is true to the families, the ethnic groups as well as to the nations. Only through enduring accumulations, can there be lasting and thriving durations.

Looking back as a traveling Chinese 30-year-living afar, I have never thought of making a mark, only writing down the experience I see and hear, and from where I personally encounter, hoping it would be useful to people who care. It would be such a joy if there are things here that folks can benefit and employ.

1 家　鄉
jiā　　xiāng

HOMETOWN

望江南 *
wàng　jiāng　nán

與你心同跳
yǔ　nǐ　xīn　tóng　tiào

2020 年 1 月 23 日

春節到 ，
chūn jiē dào

楚天驚雷爆 。
chǔ tiān jīng léi bào

人間本是歡樂酬 ，
rén jiān běn shì huān lè chóu

雞犬相聞不相邀 。
jī quǎn xiàng wén bú xiàng yāo

卻把心同跳 。
què bǎ xīn tóng tiào

新冠疫情愈發愈烈，心與武漢同在。

* 詞牌名：斜體表明是詞牌名。

1 家 鄉 HOMETOWN

1.1 *Overlooking the Yangtze River South* *

We are With You with a Silent Prayer

January 23, 2020

It's the most wonderful time of the year,

Much like the Christmas Reindeer.

Suddenly in the Southern Chu Land,

Came the spread of the pandemic fear.

A season for folks to celebrate and cheer,

No longer there for people who are near.

Painstakingly hearing from outside world,

We are with you with a silent prayer.

With the pandemic getting worse and worse, our hearts are with Wuhan.

* The italic font title indicates a metrical feature type of the classical Chinese metrical poetry.

滿　江　紅
mǎn　jiāng　hóng

戰　瘟　疫
zhàn　wēn　yì

2020　年　2　月　7　日

遙　望　九　州　，
yáo　wàng　jiǔ　zhōu

街　巷　空　、　城　郭　依　舊　。
jiē　xiàng　kōng　　chéng　guō　yī　jiù

同　胞　難　、　血　比　水　稠　，
tóng　bāo　nán　　xuè　bǐ　shuǐ　chóu

肺　裂　心　揪　。
fèi　liè　xīn　jiū

博　愛　邪　惡　或　同　源　，
bó　ài　xié　è　huò　tóng　yuán

慈　善　醜　陋　亦　共　流　。
cí　shàn　chǒu　lòu　yì　gòng　liú

權　衛　士　，
quán　wèi　shì

撕　下　假　面　具　，
sī　xià　jiǎ　miàn　jù

何　處　搜　？
hé　chù　sōu

1.2.1　*Full Red River*

Fighting the Pandemic

February 7, 2020

Looking over the divine land,

The cities with empty streets still stand.

The people are suffering,

The outside does not seem to understand.

It's hard to give them a hand,

With outside connection nearly banned.

Blood is thicker than water,

How can the fellows not apprehend?

Universal love and evil come in a band,

Charity and ugliness display even with head in the sand.

The guardians of human rights,

Why put up masks and pretend to be blind?

1.2.2

滿 江 紅
mǎn　jiāng　hóng

戰　瘟　疫
zhàn　wēn　yì

2020 年 2 月 7 日

槍 炮 棄 ， 盔 甲 丟 。
qiāng pào qì　kuī jiǎ diū

新 兵 法 ， 上 層 樓 。
xīn bīng fǎ　shàng céng lóu

待 洗 禮 ，
dài xǐ lǐ

民 族 復 興 再 就 。
mín zú fù xìng zài jiù

假 冒 偽 善 野 蠻 狂 ，
jiǎ mào wěi shàn yě mán kuáng

同 情 良 知 文 明 秀 。
tóng qíng liáng zhī wén míng xiù

開 先 河 、 逆 向 人 民 戰 ，
kāi xiān hé　nì xiàng rén mín zhàn

載 千 秋 。
zǎi qiān qiū

1.2.2 *Full Red River*

Fighting the Pandemic

February 7, 2020

With the guns and armor abandoned,

Need a new war strategy of effective command.

Combining resilience with perseverance,

The revival of the nation will come again.

Hypocritical savage is often arrogant,

Civilized compassion and conscience grow intelligent.

Look at the real issues and focus on the real efforts,

Get rid of the nonsense that is irrelevant.

With strategies and executions well planned,

Withstand a short living of a lonely island.

Unprecedent use of reverse People's war,

The victory will go down history in years of thousand.

夢　故　鄉
mèng　gù　xiāng

2020 年　3 月　3 日

夜　夢　青　山　空　中　看　，
yè　mèng　qīng　shān　kōng　zhōng　kàn

長　江　贛　江　銀　線　穿　，
cháng　jiāng　gàn　jiāng　yín　xiàn　chuān

西　圖　上　海　一　水　隔　，
xī　tú　shàng　hǎi　yī　shuǐ　gé

原　是　江　南　春　風　喚　。
yuán　shì　jiāng　nán　chūn　fēng　huàn

1.3　Hometown Dream

March 3, 2020

Dreaming about the green hills in the night,

Looking over the land from the tall sky height,

The Yangtze River and Ganjiang River,

Like two threads of silver light,

With a body of water in far sight,

Seattle and Shanghai are of similar site.

The Spring breeze from the Yangtze River south,

Blowing the Southern warm air of delight.

蘇　幕　遮
sū　mù　zhē

嫦　娥　奔　月
cháng　é　bēn　yuè

2020 年 11 月 26 日

南　海　灘　，
nán　hǎi　tān

九　天　邊　。
jiǔ　tiān　biān

嫦　娥　遠　征　，
cháng　é　yuǎn　zhēng

捎　信　吳　剛　看　。
shāo　xìn　wú　gāng　kàn

牛　郎　織　女　銀　河　歡　，
niú　láng　zhī　nǚ　yín　hé　huān

迢　迢　星　宿　，
tiáo　tiáo　xīng　xiù

難　擋　意　誌　堅　。
nán　dǎng　yì　zhì　jiān

1.4.1 *Linoleum Hat*

Chang'e Flying to the Moon

November 26, 2020

From the beach of the South China sea,
To where heaven is supposed to be,
Chang'e starts out a long expedition,
With a letter for Wu Gang to see.

In the mighty and vast galaxy,
The cowherd and weaver of the star fairy,
Excitedly waiting in the far constellation,
Welcome old friend to take a hard journey.

1.4.2　　　蘇　幕　遮
　　　　　　　sū　　mù　　zhē

嫦　娥　奔　月
cháng　é　bēn　yuè

2020 年 11 月 26 日

工　業　換　，
gōng　yè　huàn

科　技　添　。
kē　jì　tiān

神　農　千　年　，
shén　nóng　qiān　nián

人　間　再　蛻　變　。
rén　jiān　zài　tuì　biàn

時　代　弄　潮　常　快　現　，
shí　dài　nòng　cháo　cháng　kuài　xiàn

夢　想　風　流　，
mèng　xiǎng　fēng　liú

盡　在　後　生　間　。
jìn　zài　hòu　shēng　jiān

1.4.2 *Linoleum Hat*

Chang'e Flying to the Moon

November 26, 2020

With the arrival of the industrial spree,
And the science becomes the key,
Agriculture of thousands of years,
Slowly gives in its way and flee.

It's with high certainty,
Comes an era of great creativity.
The times are constantly changing,
Dreams stay with the generation of ingenuity.

1.5　　夢昆侖　　5

mèng kūn lún

居美近三十年。經歷大小布什、克林頓、奧巴馬、特朗普、拜登時代。見證分裂的民主選舉、相互鄙視的政權更替、荒唐的變性廁所、謊言漫天的極端行為。還有泛濫的毒品。每況愈下，漸感失望。

夜夢回恐龍時期，變一鳥翺翔藍天。山谷盡是花木草林、江河水溪。天際忽現大鳥恐龍，危險恐怖。便躲息於綠水青草間。又見恐龍魚鰭遊弋淺水。避而上岸，再遇恐龍鱷魚，欲逃不能。後驚醒。似是昆侖山。思來想去，填《燕山亭•昆侖》。

1.5　　　　　　Dream of Mount Kunlun

Thirty years of living in America have spanned the eras of George Bush Sr, George Bush Jr, Bill Clinton, Barack Obama, Donald Trump and Joe Biden. It has been shocking to witness the divided democratic elections, the mutual despise regime changes, the absurd transgender toilets, the extreme acts of lying and the continuing flooding of drugs. The situation is getting worse and worse and progressively and hopelessly disappointing.

A dream came up one night going back to the time of dinosaurs. I turned into a bird soaring freely in the blue sky. The huge valley was full of flowers, trees, forests, rivers and streams. Suddenly the sky was full of big birds and dinosaurs, dangerous and terrifying. I tried to hide in the shallow water and green grass, then saw dinosaur shark fins swimming in the shallow water. Escaping to ashore got into meeting dinosaurs and crocodiles again. Completely ambushed with no chance of escaping, I immediately woke up. The dream seemed to be in Mount Kunlun. Thinking it over, I started to write the poem "Pavilion of Mount Yan • Kunlun".

燕 山 亭
yàn shān tíng

昆 侖
kūn lún

2020 年 12 月 5 日

拔 地 而 起 ， 穿 空 萬 尺 ，
bá dì ér qǐ chuān kōng wàn chǐ

六 千 萬 個 冬 季 。
liù qiān wàn gè dōng jì

震 宇 母 神 ， 世 界 屋 脊 ，
zhèn yǔ mǔ shén shì jiè wū jǐ

橫 斷 天 下 東 西 。
héng duàn tiān xià dōng xī

文 明 搖 籃 ，
wén míng yáo lán

東 方 立 ， 經 久 不 息 。
dōng fāng lì jīng jiǔ bú xī

瑤 池 ，
yáo chí

三 界 九 天 歸 ， 王 母 玉 帝 。
sān jiè jiǔ tiān guī wáng mǔ yù dì

1.6.1 *Pavilion of Mount Yan*

Mount Kunlun

December 5, 2020

Arising from ground up high,

Ten thousand feet through the sky,

For sixty million ferocious winters,

The Kunlun Goddess stands never shy.

The East and West's natural divide,

The World Roof's divine pride,

Transverse through the desert and land,

The East civilization endures with long stride.

See the Jade Lake with bird view eye,

Three Realms and Nine Heavens unite,

The upper and under worlds,

All by Queen Mother and Jade Emperor's side.

1.6.2

燕　山　亭
yàn　shān　tíng

昆　侖
kūn　lún

2020　年　12　月　5　日

塞　外　帝　國　不　繼　。
sāi　wài　dì　guó　bú　jì

亞　歷　山　大　帝　，　羅　馬　消　失　。
yà　lì　shān　dà　dì　luó　mǎ　xiāo　shī

殖　民　印　第　，　埃　及　非　彼　，
zhí　mín　yìn　dì　āi　jí　fēi　bǐ

巴　比　倫　成　塵　灰　。
bā　bǐ　lún　chéng　chén　huī

工　業　革　命　，
gong　yè　gé　mìng

三　百　年　，　西　人　獨　幟　。
sān　bǎi　nián　xī　rén　dú　zhì

往　昔　，
wǎng　xī

時　間　河　，　滄　海　一　滴　。
shí　jiān　hé　cāng　hǎi　yī　dī

1.6.2 *Pavilion of Mount Yan*

Mount Kunlun

December 5, 2020

Empires to the West said Good-Bye,

Alexander the Great would sure cry,

Egypt, Rome and colonial India,

None of them could ever fly.

Babylon has no place to die,

Industrial evolution is not a lie,

For over three hundred years,

The Western had a successful try.

Time is a river flying by,

There is no way to deny,

Past is only a drop of water,

In the ocean that will never dry.

采　桑　子
cǎi　　sāng　　zǐ

少　年　中　國　叫　秦　洲
shǎo　nián　zhōng　guó　jiào　qín　zhōu

2020　年　12　月　19　日

五　千　年　更　名　換　首　。
wǔ　qiān　nián　gèng　míng　huàn　shǒu

域　外　巷　陌　，　塞　上　關　頭　，
yù　wài　xiàng　mò　　　sāi　shàng　guān　tóu

萬　國　言　語　皆　同　口　。
wàn　guó　yán　yǔ　jiē　tóng　kǒu

古　老　東　方　盛　絲　綢　。
gǔ　lǎo　dōng　fāng　shèng　sī　chóu

不　是　瓷　器　，　更　非　清　朝　，
bú　shì　cí　qì　　　gèng　fēi　qing　cháo

少　年　中　國　叫　秦　洲　。
shǎo　nián　zhōng　guó　jiào　qín　zhōu

瓷器(china) 一千多年，清朝(Qing)出現也就四百年前。域外稱東方古國為 Cina、China。本意當為秦洲。就像 Asia、Africa 和 America 指亞洲、非洲和美洲一樣。

1.7　*Mulberry Picking*

Youth China is Called Qin

December 19, 2020

Through the five-thousand-year history,

A new name is born with a rebel victory,

Over the border or in the foreign streets,

All use the same name for the East territory.

The ancient East was a silk factory,

It's not porcelain nor Qing Dynasty,

Youth China is called Qin,

The only name in the world for its glory.

Porcelain (china) was invented more than a thousand years ago. Qing Dynasty was only 400 years old. The ancient big East country has been called Cina and China in the outside world. The original meaning should be the continent Qin, just like Asia, Africa and America

.

南 歌 子
nán　　gē　　zǐ

思 故 鄉
sī　　gù　　xiāng

2021 年 11 月 29 日

雲　上　總　太　陽　，
yún　shàng　zǒng　tài　yáng

雲　下　有　陽　光　。
yún　xià　yǒu　yáng　guāng

不　僅　夏　天　是　天　堂　。
bú　jǐn　xià　tiān　shì　tiān　táng

四　季　溫　和　如　春　、　西　村　棒　。
sì　jì　wēn　hé　rú　chūn　xī　cūn　bàng

清　酒　自　日　人　，
qīng　jiǔ　zì　rì　rén

始　覺　有　印　象　。
shǐ　jiào　yǒu　yìn　xiàng

米　酒　老　酒　家　鄉　釀　。
mǐ　jiǔ　lǎo　jiǔ　jiā　xiāng　niàng

得　一　觴　於　異　國　、　舍　熊　掌　。
dé　yī　shāng　yú　yì　guó　shě　xióng　zhǎng

1.8 *Song of the South*

Hometown Longing

November 29, 2021

There is always Sun above the cloud,

Sun shines on ground if only allowed,

Not just Seattle's paradise summer,

Mild four seasons make hometown proud.

Sake of Japan is loved by the crowd,

It almost needs to be bowed,

The same flavor of old hometown brew,

Would not trade it even if a city is vowed.

為辟邪除災、迎祥納福，古人
wéi pì xié chú zāi　yíng xiáng nà fú　gǔ rén

造桃符，置門上。桃符桃木所製，
zào táo fú　zhì mén shàng　táo fú táo mù suǒ zhì

刻神像神名，周代時就已出現。
kè shén xiàng shén míng　zhōu dài shí jiù yǐ chū xiàn

五代，桃符漸用聯語。宋時始
wǔ dài　táo fú jiàn yòng lián yǔ　sòng shí shǐ

寫對聯，亦用紅紙。明初時，春聯
xiě duì lián　yì yòng hóng zhǐ　míng chū shí　chūn lián

一詞始出。由此，春聯源於五代，
yī cí shǐ chū　yóu cǐ　chūn lián yuán yú wǔ dài

興於宋代，盛於明代，沿襲至今。
xìng yú sòng dài　shèng yú míng dài　yán xí zhì jīn

域外有迷思，以春聯和逾越節
yù wài yǒu mí sī　yǐ chūn lián hé yú yuè jiē

有聯。實非如此。羊血逾越在三千
yǒu lián　shí fēi rú cǐ　yáng xuè yú yuè zài sān qiān

五百年前埃及。桃符始四千年前，
wǔ bǎi nián qián āi jí　táo fú shǐ sì qiān nián qián

且非紅色。
qiě fēi hóng sè

春聯是中華傳統。為教師的父
chūn lián shì zhōng huá chuán tǒng　wéi jiāo shī de fù

親常讓寫對聯。家鄉有一老宅，每
qīn cháng ràng xiě duì lián　jiā xiāng yǒu yī lǎo zhái　měi

逢春節，必貼春聯，直到如今。
féng chūn jiē　bì tiē chūn lián　zhí dào rú jīn

1.9　　　　The Tradition of Spring Festival Couplet

To ward off evil spirits and disasters, and welcome blessings and prosperity, the ancient Chinese made use of a Peach Talisman and put it on the door. The Peach Talisman was made of peach wood, engraved with the names and images of the Gods. The Peach Talisman has already appeared in the Zhou Dynasty.

In the era of the Five Dynasties, the Peach Talisman started to use the coupling language. By the Song Dynasty, the couplet on the red paper was used. In the early Ming Dynasty, the phrase of Spring Festival Couplet started to appear. Thus, the Spring Festival Couplet originated from the Five Dynasties, prospered in the Song Dynasty and flourished in the Ming Dynasty, and has been inherited to this day.

There is a myth outside of China that the Sprint Festival Couplet and Jewish Passover were somehow related since both practices were similar in using the red signals around the door. It is not the case. Passover using sheep's blood occurred 3,500 years ago in Egypt while the Peach Talisman started to appear 4,000 years ago, and the Peach Talisman was not red.

Spring Festival Couplet is a Chinese tradition. As a teacher, my father let all our kids write couplets for the Spring Festival. There is an old house in my hometown. Every Spring Festival, Spring Festival couplets must be posted around the door, even until today.

春　聯
chūn　lián

1

地　靈　事　成
dì　líng　shì　chéng

對　門　山　山　不　在　高　有　山　就　靈
duì　mén　shān　shān　bú　zài　gāo　yǒu　shān　jiù　líng

土　庫　裏　理　勿　須　深　稍　理　即　成
tǔ　kù　lǐ　lǐ　wù　xū　shēn　shāo　lǐ　jí　chéng

對門山：山名

土庫裏：地名

1.10　　　　　Couplet of the Spring Festival

1

Land of the Bright and Home of the Brilliant

Mount Face-to-Face Gate,

Thou not tall,

It's the land of the bright.

Community Land Warehouse,

Thou rationale light,

It's the home of the brilliant.

春　聯
chūn　lián

2

夢　回　心　歸
mèng　huí　xīn　guī

袁　河　水　通　贛　江　融　長　江　終　匯　大　海
yuán　hé　shuǐ　tōng　gàn　jiāng　róng　cháng　jiāng　zhōng　huì　dà　hǎi

遊　子　心　鬧　他　鄉　飄　四　方　仍　歸　故　裏
yóu　zǐ　xīn　nào　tā　xiāng　piāo　sì　fāng　réng　guī　gù　lǐ

袁河、贛江：江西河流名

土庫裏：地名

1.11   Couplet of the Spring Festival

2

Home in Dream and Return in Mind

Water of the Yuan River,

Connecting to the Gan River,

Merging into the Yangtze River,

Eventually flows into ocean.

Mind of the traveler,

Making ways as a foreigner,

Journeying to the world as a wander,

Still returns home.

春　聯
chūn　lián

3

家　和　萬　事　興
jiā　hé　wàn　shì　xìng

山　以　石　竣　海　為　川　歸
shān　yǐ　shí　jùn　hǎi　wéi　chuān　guī

雪　遇　春　瑞　門　任　福　臨
xuě　yù　chūn　ruì　mén　rèn　fú　lín

1.12　　Couplet of the Spring Festival

3

Family Gets Prosperous Through Union

Mountain is complete,

When there are stones on top.

Ocean is home,

When there are rivers flowing in.

Snow is propitious,

When it meets Spring.

Blessing is arriving in,

When there are doors open.

4

家　鄉　如　此　多　嬌
jiā　xiāng　rú　cǐ　duō　jiāo

對　門　山　袁　河　水　山　青　水　綠　氣　象　新
duì　mén　shān　yuán　hé　shuǐ　shān　qīng　shuǐ　lù　qì　xiàng　xīn

袁　匯　渠　石　頭　城　渠　長　城　堅　地　方　好
yuán　huì　qú　shí　tóu　chéng　qú　cháng　chéng　jiān　dì　fāng　hǎo

袁河：江西河流名

袁匯渠：水渠名

石頭城、城頭：同一地名

1.13　Couplet of the Spring Festival

4

Hometown is so Beautiful

Mount Gate Face-to-Face,

The Yuan River,

Mountain is emerald, and river is green,

There is a new horizon.

Stone City,

The Yuan canal,

The city is strong, and the canal is long,

There is a great place for hometown.

春　聯
chūn　lián

5

萬　象　更　新
wàn　xiàng　gèng　xīn

春　色　染　城　頭　山　河　千　載　秀
chūn　sè　rǎn　chéng　tóu　shān　hé　qiān　zǎi　xiù

東　風　拂　對　門　大　地　萬　裏　豐
dōng　fēng　fú　duì　mén　dà　dì　wàn　lǐ　fēng

城頭、對門：地名

1.14　　　Couplet of the Spring Festival

5

All Things Change from Old to New

The color of Spring,

Painting the Stone City,

The rivers and mountains,

Showing the thousand-year beauty.

The warmth of wind,

Blowing the Gate Face-to-Face,

The earth and the world,

Displaying ten-thousand-mile abundance.

1.15　春　聯
　　chūn　lián

6

和　諧　秀　美
hé　xié　xiù　měi

天　和　地　和　人　和　和　融　故　裏
tiān　hé　dì　hé　rén　hé　hé　róng　gù　lǐ

山　美　水　美　心　美　美　在　鄉　間
shān　měi　shuǐ　měi　xīn　měi　měi　zài　xiāng　jiān

1.15　　　Couplet of the Spring Festival

6

Melodious Harmony and Elegant Beauty

Heaven is harmonious,

Earth is melodious,

People are united,

Hometown is bonded peacefully.

Mountains are elegant,

Waters are beautiful,

Hearts are sweet,

The countryside is tendered magnificently.

7

風　和　氣　瑞
fēng　hé　qì　ruì

袁　水　邊　沙　洲　外　春　風　悄　悄　來
yuán　shuǐ　biān　shā　zhōu　wài　chūn　fēng　qiāo　qiāo　lái

山　嶺　上　門　田　間　喜　氣　處　處　在
shān　lǐng　shàng　mén　tián　jiān　xǐ　qì　chù　chù　zài

袁水：河名

沙洲、嶺上、門田：地名

1.16　　Couplet of the Spring Festival

7

Mild Wind and Auspicious Pattern

Along the side of the Yuan River,

Beyond the sandbar,

The Spring breeze is coming quietly.

Over at the mountains,

Among the fields and gardens,

The festival joy is spreading immensely.

春　聯
chūn　lián

8

丹　心　矢　誌
dān　xīn　shǐ　zhì

盡　吾　誌　而　不　能　至　者　可　以　無　悔
jìn　wú　zhì　ér　bú　néng　zhì　zhě　kě　yǐ　wú　huǐ

窮　丹　心　而　未　有　報　者　仍　處　無　憂
qióng　dān　xīn　ér　wèi　yǒu　bào　zhě　réng　chù　wú　yōu

1.17　Couplet of the Spring Festival

8

Dedication and Determination

Those who are determined,

Who have done their best,

Who can't yet arrive where it's expected,

Can have no regret.

Those who are dedicated,

Who have been most loyal,

Who haven't yet served their country,

Can have no fret.

春　　聯
chūn　　lián

9

濃　濃　新　春　喜　氣　洋　洋
nóng　nóng　xīn　chūn　xǐ　qì　yáng　yáng

春　風　來　飛　紅　萬　點　喜　如　海
chūn　fēng　lái　fēi　hóng　wàn　diǎn　xǐ　rú　hǎi

新　潮　湧　波　濤　萬　頃　氣　如　虹
xīn　cháo　yǒng　bō　tāo　wàn　qǐng　qì　rú　hóng

1.18   Couplet of the Spring Festival

9

Immersing Spring Festival Radiant with Joy

The Spring breeze is coming,

Blowing off thousands of red flowers,

Bringing a sea of joy.

The new tide is surging,

Forming up thousands of rushing waves,

Washing away the history.

春　聯
chūn　lián

10

徑　新　直　遂
jìng　xīn　zhí　suí

新　年　新　天　新　日　子　樣　樣　新
xīn　nián　xīn　tiān　xīn　rì　zǐ　yàng　yàng　xīn

順　風　順　路　順　時　代　事　事　順
shùn　fēng　shùn　lù　shùn　shí　dài　shì　shì　shùn

1.19　Couplet of the Spring Festival

10

New Path Straight and Smooth

New year,

New day,

New time,

Everything is new.

Favorable wind,

Favorable road,

Favorable era,

Plain sailing is favorable.

2 青春

qing chūn

YOUTH

千　秋　歲
qiān　qiū　suì

青　春　頌
qīng　chūn　sòng

2019　年　10　月　11　日

香　山　葉　紅　，　京　都　秋　色　濃　。
xiāng　shān　yè　hóng　　jīng　dū　qiū　sè　nóng

單　車　騎　，　長　城　沖　。
dān　chē　qí　　cháng　chéng　chōng

蘇　州　街　胡　同　，　築　起　青　春　夢　。
sū　zhōu　jiē　hú　tóng　　zhù　qǐ　qīng　chūn　mèng

瞅　閑　空　，　竊　遊　頤　園　十　七　孔　。
chǒu　xián　kōng　　qiè　yóu　yí　yuán　shí　qī　kǒng

七　年　北　京　撞　，　四　處　留　行　蹤　。
qī　nián　běi　jīng　zhuàng　　sì　chù　liú　xíng　zōng

別　淚　崩　，　光　陰　送　。
bié　lèi　bēng　　guāng　yīn　sòng

但　願　越　時　空　，　回　到　燕　園　中　。
dàn　yuàn　yuè　shí　kōng　　huí　dào　yàn　yuán　zhōng

琴　弦　動　，　響　起　阿　罕　布　拉　宮　。
qín　xián　dòng　　xiǎng　qǐ　ā　hǎn　bù　lā　gōng

2　青　春　YOUTH

2.1　*Year of Thousand Autumns*

Ode to Youth

October 11, 2019

The leaves on Mt Fragrance turning red,

Beijing's thick Autumn is well bred,

Ride a bike and climb the Great Wall,

A youthful dream looms in the head.

Good words spread,

Nice places to tread,

Not just palaces and alley ways,

Seven years of wonder fast sped.

College studies are a dread,

Light has well been shed,

Wish to bring the past to the future,

Turn Alhambra melody into a forever thread.

沁　園　春
qìn　yuán　chūn

傳　奇　的　旋　律
chuán　qí　de　xuán　lù

2019　年　12　月　3　日

大　學　閑　暇　，　試　練　吉　它　，
dà　xué　xián　xiá　　shì　liàn　jí　tā

恨　天　賦　差　。
hèn　tiān　fù　chà

弗　拉　門　戈　曲　，　難　度　猶　大　，
fú　lā　mén　gē　qǔ　　nán　dù　yóu　dà

手　笨　技　拙　，　勿　能　彈　下　。
shǒu　bèn　jì　zhuō　　wù　néng　tán　xià

大　師　演　奏　，　令　人　淚　灑　，
dà　shī　yǎn　zòu　　lìng　rén　lèi　sǎ

如　《　角　鬥　士　》　西　班　伢　。
rú　　jiǎo　dòu　shì　　xī　bān　yá

不　信　邪　，　領　千　軍　萬　馬　，
bú　xìn　xié　　lǐng　qiān　jūn　wàn　mǎ

奮　力　廝　殺　。
fèn　lì　sī　shā

2.2.1 *Spring of Refreshing Garden*

The Melody of a Legend

December 3, 2019

At the spare time in college square,

Tried to play the classic guitar,

Blame self for lack of talent,

Flamenco is truly as hard as green card.

Hands are clumsy and skills are apart,

Better turn to the legendary master,

The extraordinary performance,

Would sure make people shed tear.

Like leading thousands of troops in a war,

The Espanola in the Gladiator,

No nonsense or do not give a hang,

To survive you have to fight hard.

2.2.2

沁 園 春
qìn yuán chūn

傳 奇 的 旋 律
chuán qí de xuán lù

2019 年 12 月 3 日

阿 斯 圖 裏 亞 斯 ，
ā sī tú lǐ yà sī

譜 寫 禦 敵 抗 爭 神 話 。
pǔ xiě yù dí kàng zhēng shén huà

多 少 同 樣 事 ， 天 地 不 仁 ，
duō shǎo tóng yàng shì tiān dì bú rén

外 族 騷 淩 ， 屢 臨 中 華 。
wài zú sāo líng lǚ lín zhōng huá

千 年 上 下 ， 萬 裏 遼 闊 ，
qiān nián shàng xià wàn lǐ liáo kuò

風 雪 裏 成 長 壯 大 。
fēng xuě lǐ chéng zhǎng zhuàng dà

看 如 今 ， 似 狼 纏 虎 嚇 ，
kàn rú jīn sì láng chán hǔ xià

有 何 懼 怕 ？
yǒu hé jù pà

2.2.2 *Spring of Refreshing Garden*

The Melody of a Legend

December 3, 2019

The classical masterpiece of Asturias leyenda,

A story of fending the enemy without fear,

Determination wins the ultimate victory,

History is amazingly similar.

Heaven and Earth do not care,

Gunboat policy and the threat of warfare,

In hundreds of years of an unusual era,

Repeatedly entangled the weak China.

Ten thousand miles and millennia,

Adversity is a good sparring partner,

Facing an encircling wolf pack and a tiger,

Why would there be scare if there is no fear?

行香子
xíng　xiāng　zǐ

六〇七〇後
liù　líng　qī　líng　hòu

2020 年 4 月 18 日

三　年　災　害　，　下　鄉　應　派　。
sān　nián　zāi　hài　　xià　xiāng　yīng　pài

幸　運　孩　，　恰　逢　避　開　。
xìng　yùn　hái　　qià　féng　bì　kāi

公　金　助　學　，　職　位　分　配　。
gōng　jīn　zhù　xué　　zhí　wèi　fèn　pèi

童　年　歡　快　，　彈　弓　射　，　鐵　環　推　。
tóng　nián　huān　kuài　　dàn　gōng　shè　　tiě　huán　tuī

篤　信　真　愛　，　信　念　心　懷　。
dǔ　xìn　zhēn　ài　　xìn　niàn　xīn　huái

引　思　潮　，　國　學　胸　揣　。
yǐn　sī　cháo　　guó　xué　xiōng　chuāi

傳　承　革　新　，　兼　收　進　改　。
chuán　chéng　gé　xīn　　jiān　shōu　jìn　gǎi

信　息　世　界　，　開　拓　者　，　領　時　代　。
xìn　xī　shì　jiè　　kāi　tuò　zhě　　lǐng　shí　dài

2.3 *Rite of Burning Incense*

Generation of 1960's & 1970's

April 18, 2020

Three-year natural disasters nationwide,

Movement of going to the countryside,

Lucky generation of educated youth,

Narrowly dodging the political tide.

Guaranteed job and free college ride,

No need to put childhood joys aside,

With ideals and beliefs and faith in true love,

Leading the thought trend of popular ride.

When old and new collide,

Never let new ideas slide,

Melting tradition with creation,

Being a pioneer with the information era pride.

3 大　學
dà　xué

COLLEGE

千　秋　歲
qiān　qiū　suì

燕　園　夢　懷
yàn　yuán　mèng　huái

2019　年　8　月　28　日

河　邊　洲　外　，　　城　頭　春　意　來　。
hé　biān　zhōu　wài　　chéng　tóu　chūn　yì　lái

鳥　聲　悅　，　　百　花　開　。
niǎo　shēng　yuè　　bǎi　huā　kāi

祖　母　眼　中　盼　，　　新　溪　三　年　曬　。
zǔ　mǔ　yǎn　zhōng　pàn　　xīn　xī　sān　nián　shài

挑　燈　夜　，　　丹　心　銳　誌　似　猶　在　。
tiāo　dēng　yè　　dān　xīn　ruì　zhì　sì　yóu　zài

三　年　新　余　快　，　　青　春　新　一　代　。
sān　nián　xīn　yú　kuài　　qīng　chūn　xīn　yī　dài

雁　北　飛　，　　京　都　邁　。
yàn　běi　fēi　　jīng　dū　mài

燕　園　青　夢　懷　，　　癡　心　仍　未　改　。
yàn　yuán　qīng　mèng　huái　　chī　xīn　réng　wèi　gǎi

行　李　帶　，　　為　求　功　名　渡　大　海　。
xíng　lǐ　dài　　wéi　qiú　gōng　míng　dù　dà　hǎi

城頭：出生地　　　新溪：初中上學地　　　新余：高中上學地

3.1　*Year of Thousand Autumns*

The Dream of Garden Yan

August 28, 2019

Beyond the sandbar and along the river,
Spring comes to Chengtou dispelling the winter.
Birds are singing and flowers are blooming,
Grandmother's glittering eyes for a thriving year.

Three years of hard work in Xinxi prove no quitter.
The persistence seems to still be there.
Three years of Xinyu comes a youth generation.
The goslings fly north even in December.

Dream in the Garden Yan could last forever.
The infatuation and passion do not shiver.
To pursue the ultimate ambition,
Willing to cross the ocean and go wherever.

Chengtou: Birthplace　　Xinxin: Junior High　　Xinyu: Senior High

3.2　　　丁　石　孫　校　長　　　24
　　　　　dīng　shí　sūn　xiào　zhǎng

　　　　2019　年　10　月　12　日

　　　　身　為　數　學　家　，
　　　　shēn　wéi　shù　xué　jiā
　　　　心　裝　滿　天　下　。
　　　　xīn　zhuāng　mǎn　tiān　xià
　　　　教　育　治　學　大　，
　　　　jiāo　yù　zhì　xué　dà
　　　　師　者　學　子　誇　。
　　　　shī　zhě　xué　zǐ　kuā

　　　　垂　範　後　世　嘉　，
　　　　chuí　fàn　hòu　shì　jiā
　　　　見　證　巨　變　化　。
　　　　jiàn　zhèng　jù　biàn　huà
　　　　人　格　留　佳　話　，
　　　　rén　gé　liú　jiā　huà
　　　　照　亮　博　雅　塔　。
　　　　zhào　liàng　bó　yǎ　tǎ

北京時間 2019 年 10 月 12 日，在校時校長丁石孫先生逝世。聞此消息時，剛填完詞《千秋歲‧青春》（原為紀念入北大 35 周年），心中突感無限失落。逝去的不僅是我們的青春，還有我們的校長。國學大師季羨林曾說，北大有兩位校長應長鳴歷史，一是蔡元培，另一是丁石孫。謹以此詩紀念丁石孫校長。

3.2

Beida President Shisun Ding

October 12, 2019

Trained is a mathematics professional.

The love for his country has captured his soul.

Education and academia are always his goal.

The teachers and the students all have made it whole.

Setting a great example and a role model,

In times when paradigm shifts, and changes unroll.

With characters and integrity shining later generations,

Leading the great school as the standing high flagpole.

On October 12, 2019, Beijing Standard Time, College time Beida President Shisun Ding passed away. This occurred right after finishing the poem "The Year of Thousand Autumns • Ode to Youth". There was a feeling of unlimited loss and infinite void. We forever lost our youth, and our President of Beida, Chinese Culture and Sinology Master, Beida Professor Xianlin Ji once said, there are two prominent Beida Presidents who will go down in history and will forever be remembered. One is Yuanpei Cai. The other one is Shisun Ding. This poem is dedicated to remembering President Shisun Ding.

憶　江　南
yì　jiāng　nán

北　國　之　秋
běi　guó　zhī　qiū

2019　年　10　月　31　日

城　郭　望　，
chéng　guō　wàng

滿　眼　盡　金　黃　。
mǎn　yǎn　jìn　jīn　huáng

長　城　蜿　蜒　五　彩　洋　，
cháng　chéng　wān　yán　wǔ　cǎi　yáng

重　巒　起　伏　層　波　浪　。
chóng　luán　qǐ　fú　céng　bō　làng

秋　把　美　圖　張　。
qiū　bǎ　měi　tú　zhāng

北國：北京，長城，波士頓，西雅圖

3.3　*Reminiscing the Yangtze River South*

Autumn of the Northern Lands

October 31, 2019

Looking out beyond the city hall,

Seeing the golden colors of the Fall.

The colorful vegetation acts like the meandering ocean.

Only when it's in the Fall and you climb the Great Wall.

Beijing, Seattle, or wherever you stroll,

Overlapping mountains or bustling shore,

Undulating wave of natural scenery,

Autumn paints the picture and makes it all.

The Northern Lands: Beijing, The Great Wall, Boston, Seattle

憶　秦　娥
yì　qín　é

阿　斯　圖　裏　亞　斯　的　傳　奇
ā　sī　tú　lǐ　yà　sī　de　chuán　qí

2019　年　12　月　1　日

西　北　部　，
xī　běi　bù

西　班　牙　人　抗　征　服　。
xī　bān　yá　rén　kàng　zhēng　fú

抗　征　服　，
kàng　zhēng　fú

金　戈　鐵　馬　，　沙　場　深　處　。
jīn　gē　tiě　mǎ　　shā　chǎng　shēn　chù

不　屈　不　饒　傳　奇　訴　，
bú　qū　bú　ráo　chuán　qí　sù

屢　戰　還　勇　不　畏　懼　。
lǚ　zhàn　hái　yǒng　bú　wèi　jù

不　畏　懼　，
bú　wèi　jù

河　山　依　在　，　腥　風　飄　絮　。
hé　shān　yī　zài　　xīng　fēng　piāo　xù

《阿斯圖裏亞斯的傳奇》是大學時彈的一首古典吉它曲。

3.4　*Reminiscing the Princess of Qin*

The Legend of Asturias

December 1, 2019

Up in Asturias of Spain's Northwest,

The Spanish resisted the conquest.

Resisted the hardest conquest.

Horses and spears, swords and shields,

The will to fend off enemy was the strongest.

The legend of unyielding was put to test.

The hardest battle brought out the best.

Brought out the very best.

Territory still stood in the bloody battlefield.

The victory belonged to the bravest.

"The Legend of Asturias" is a classic guitar piece played when in college.

未　名　湖
wèi　míng　hú

2020　年　10　月　2　日

柳　下　水　邊　琴　聲　留　，
liǔ　xià　shuǐ　biān　qín　shēng　liú

愛　也　深　秋　，　淚　也　深　秋　。
ài　yě　shēn　qiū　　lèi　yě　shēn　qiū

石　舟　不　渡　湖　心　丘　，
shí　zhōu　bú　dù　hú　xīn　qiū

不　做　冕　旒　，　勝　做　冕　旒　。
bú　zuò　miǎn　liú　　shèng　zuò　miǎn　liú

紅　樓　塔　影　映　自　由　，
hóng　lóu　tǎ　yǐng　yìng　zì　yóu

小　徑　任　遊　，　小　橋　任　遊　。
xiǎo　jìng　rèn　yóu　　xiǎo　qiáo　rèn　yóu

青　春　無　羈　不　知　愁　，
qīng　chūn　wú　jī　bú　zhī　chóu

愛　上　層　樓　，　易　上　層　樓　。
ài　shàng　céng　lóu　　yì　shàng　céng　lóu

3.5 *Twig of Plum Blossom*

Lake No Name

October 2, 2020

The willow is dancing like a new wed bride,

With the music of guitar for the lake stride.

Love in Autumn and tears in Autumn,

The stone boat never crosses to the other side.

Red house and Pagoda act like a guide,

Glittering freely in the water well aligned.

Not being powerful but better than powerful.

Pathways and bridges do not need to be wide.

Why let worry and concern hide?

There are ways for rules to abide.

Love to climb a floor and easy to climb a floor,

The vigor of youth should never subside.

4 留　學

liú　　xué

STUDY ABROAD

千　　秋　　歲
qiān　　qiū　　suì

一　路　走　來
yī　lù　zǒu　lái

2019　年　12　月　31　日

海　邊　山　外　，　東　西　兩　岸　呆　。
hǎi　biān　shān　wài　　dōng　xī　liǎng　àn　dāi

波　城　帥　，　康　橋　愛　。
bō　chéng　shuài　　kāng　qiáo　ài

五　年　潛　心　鑽　，　新　時　不　我　待　。
wǔ　nián　qián　xīn　zuàn　　xīn　shí　bú　wǒ　dài

長　車　奔　，　躊　躇　滿　誌　西　部　開　。
cháng　chē　bēn　　chóu　chú　mǎn　zhì　xī　bù　kāi

潮　流　變　化　快　，　昔　事　多　不　在　。
cháo　liú　biàn　huà　kuài　　xī　shì　duō　bú　zài

物　更　新　，　似　比　賽　。
wù　gèng　xīn　　sì　bǐ　sài

南　北　四　處　闖　，　西　村　廿　三　載　。
nán　běi　sì　chù　chuǎng　　xī　cūn　niàn　sān　zǎi

朱　顏　改　，　一　路　走　來　重　感　慨　。
zhū　yán　gǎi　　yī　lù　zǒu　lái　zhòng　gǎn　kǎi

4.1 *Year of Thousand Autumns*

Come All the Way

December 31, 2019

Over the mountains and beside the sea,

From coast to coast where we love to be.

Boston is handsome, and Cambridge is awesome.

Five years of hard study barely with time free.

In an era that no one would wait for me,

Long drive to the west with no guarantee.

Time is changing fast, and things fade from past.

Adapting to the new world becomes the key.

To North and South with gloom and glee,

Twenty-three years in Seattle fly in a cup of tea.

Things come and go as in a game show,

Seeing it all is amazing with silver hair upon thee.

永　遇　樂
yǒng　yù　lè

馬　薩　諸　塞　的　劍　橋
mǎ　sà　zhū　sāi　de　jiàn　qiáo

2021　年　1　月　7　日

仁　立　美　洲　，　　海　岸　東　頭　，
zhù　lì　měi　zhōu　　hǎi　àn　dōng　tóu

大　西　洋　角　。
dà　xī　yáng　jiǎo

新　英　格　蘭　，　　依　然　昂　首　，
xīn　yīng　gé　lán　　yī　rán　áng　shǒu

不　列　顛　驕　傲　。
bú　liè　diān　jiāo　ào

普　利　茅　斯　，　　五　月　花　號　，
pǔ　lì　máo　sī　　wǔ　yuè　huā　hào

引　來　反　叛　清　教　。
yǐn　lái　fǎn　pàn　qīng　jiāo

誰　曾　想　、　獨　立　一　槍　，
shuí　céng　xiǎng　　dú　lì　yī　qiāng

鑄　就　帝　國　今　朝　。
zhù　jiù　dì　guó　jīn　zhào

新英格蘭: New England，美國東北地区。五月花號: 英國清教徒來到美洲的第一條船，登陸麻州的普利茅斯。獨立第一槍: 波士頓郊外的列克星敦的對英戰爭，奠定了美國的獨立。麻省大道: Massachusetts Avenue.　查爾斯河: Charles River.

4.2.1 *Where it Forever Meets Glee*

Cambridge of Massachusetts

January 17, 2021

Standing in the land of America,

Facing the East to the Cape Cod,

In a quiet Atlantic corner,

Ever holding the head high,

Always seen as bright.

New England is still a British honor.

Sailing the Mayflower,

Arriving in harsh winter,

From Plymouth to Plymouth,

Barely surviving the nature's devour.

Who would have thought?

Coming with it is a superpower.

4.2.2

永　遇　樂
yǒng　yù　lè

馬　薩　諸　塞　的　劍　橋
mǎ　sà　zhū　sāi　de　jiàn　qiáo

2021　年　1　月　7　日

查　爾　斯　河　，　麻　省　大　道　，
chá　ěr　sī　hé　　má　shěng　dà　dào

熙　攘　不　讓　靜　悄　。
xī　rǎng　bú　ràng　jìng　qiāo

跨　哈　佛　橋　，　過　朗　費　羅　，
kuà　hā　fó　qiáo　　guò　lǎng　fèi　luó

波　城　通　劍　橋　。
bō　chéng　tōng　jiàn　qiáo

冬　去　夏　到　，　河　上　劃　艇　，
dōng　qù　xià　dào　　hé　shàng　huá　tǐng

似　南　國　龍　舟　飆　。
sì　nán　guó　lóng　zhōu　biāo

長　漫　思　、　無　限　長　廊　，
cháng　màn　sī　　wú　xiàn　cháng　láng

常　春　藤　條　。
cháng　chūn　téng　tiáo

哈佛橋：Harvard Bridge; 朗費羅：Longfellow Bridge; 無限長廊：
Infinity Corridor of MIT；常春藤：Ivy，多現東部悠久學樓。波城：
Boston （半年冬天，直接入夏）；劍橋：Cambridge，以英國劍橋大
學命名的麻州城市。

4.2.2 *Where it Forever Meets Glee*

Cambridge of Massachusetts

January 17, 2021

The silent Charles River,

Evermore a generous giver.

The downtown hustle and bustle,

Not yielding to campus nestle,

Bridges of Harvard and Longfellow,

Connecting the world to the ivory tower.

Winter goes to the summer.

Rowing comes back to the water.

Feeling like dragon boat race,

And the Southern land's fast pace.

Thinking of the infinite corridor,

And ivy climbing wall like a warrior.

卜　算　子
bǔ　　suàn　　zǐ

詠　梅
yǒng　méi

2021　年　3　月　3　日

不　爭　芳　艷　濃　，
bú　zhēng　fāng　yàn　nóng

獨　異　百　花　叢　。
dú　yì　bǎi　huā　cóng

傲　霜　鬥　雪　春　信　傳　，
ào　shuāng　dòu　xuě　chūn　xìn　chuán

捷　足　把　冬　送　。
jié　zú　bǎ　dōng　sòng

哈　佛　商　課　重　，
hā　fó　shāng　kè　zhòng

案　例　堆　如　嵩　。
àn　lì　duī　rú　sōng

挑　燈　猶　須　跳　越　讀　，
tiāo　dēng　yóu　xū　tiào　yuè　dú

問　時　沙　場　沖　。
wèn　shí　shā　chǎng　chōng

4.3 *Divination Minor*

Ode to the Plum Blossom

March 3, 2021

Indifferent of being colorful and fragrant,
Never showing up in events that are extravagant.
Enduring bitter frost and fighting harsh snow,
Sending off winter as the Spring agent.

Case studies of business class are so frequent.
Mission impossible to keep reading current.
Pick the first and last sections that are important.
First one in class to tell what is apparent.

蔔　算　子
bǔ　suàn　zǐ

話　梅
huà　méi

2021　年　3　月　3　日

天　性　喜　出　眾　，
tiān　xìng　xǐ　chū　zhòng

不　與　百　花　同　。
bú　yǔ　bǎi　huā　tóng

愛　哭　嬰　孩　有　奶　吃　，
ài　kū　yīng　hái　yǒu　nǎi　chī

出　奇　先　爭　寵　。
chū　qí　xiān　zhēng　chǒng

案　例　不　易　懂　，
àn　lì　bú　yì　dǒng

前　排　早　沒　空　。
qián　pái　zǎo　méi　kōng

只　為　印　象　好　成　績　，
zhǐ　wéi　yìn　xiàng　hǎo　chéng　jì

近　水　樓　臺　擁　。
jìn　shuǐ　lóu　tái　yōng

哈佛案例方法，閱讀是不可能完成任務。堆積如山的個案分析，不睡覺也讀不完。如何脫穎而出，是八仙過海，各顯神通。若要拔群出萃，就得別出心裁。

4.4 *Divination Minor*

Plum Blossom

March 3, 2021

Natural born standing out of crowd,

More often than not thinking out loud,

Like crying baby always getting milk,

Tricks and ways to get things allowed.

Case studies too many to be plowed,

First rows of class always early out.

To get good impression and good grade,

Answer easy questions first just to stand out.

"The Harvard Case Study Method" is a mission impossible task for a business class. There is not sufficient time for students to complete the reading for the cases. To achieve good impression and grades, students employ all kinds of tricks and ways to impress professors.

5 工　作
gōng　zuò

WORK

探　春　令
tàn　chūn　lìng

重　返　紐　約
chóng　fǎn　niǔ　yuē

2019　年　3　月　27　日

匆　匆　我　來　，　急　急　而　走　，
cōng　cōng　wǒ　lái　　jí　jí　ér　zǒu

暖　陽　和　色　。
nuǎn　yáng　hé　sè

攜　西　村　櫻　花　，　柔　柔　春　光　，
xié　xī　cūn　yīng　huā　　róu　róu　chūn　guāng

短　假　猶　閑　樂　。
duǎn　jiǎ　yóu　xián　lè

八　時　外　松　馳　透　徹　。
bā　shí　wài　sōng　chí　tòu　chè

滋　滋　念　想　著　。
zī　zī　niàn　xiǎng　zhe

隨　都　市　人　流　，　慢　慢　的　我　，
suí　dū　shì　rén　liú　　màn　màn　de　wǒ

半　個　紐　約　客　。
bàn　gè　niǔ　yuē　kè

西村：Seattle 西雅圖

紐約客：New Yorker 紐約人

5　工作　WORK

5.1　*Short Tune of Spring Exploration*

Return to New York

March 27, 2019

Hastily I arrive, just like hurriedly I leave.
At daughter's spring break chime,
I bring the warm Seattle Spring sunshine,
And the cherry blossom of the gentle kind,
To the perfect town and at the perfect time.

The constant thought in the mind,
The good relaxation beyond nine to five.
Jump on the bandwagon of city trend,
Day in and out leaving transit behind.
Being a New Yorker shifts paradigm.

千秋歲
qiān　qiū　suì

底特律的秋日
dǐ　tè　lù　de　qiū　rì

2019 年 9 月 11 日

通用福特，加克萊斯勒。
tōng yòng fú tè　jiā kè lái sī lè

昔日夢，今日惻。
xī rì mèng　jīn rì cè

開艷羨汽車，住郊外房舍。
kāi yàn xiàn qì chē　zhù jiāo wài fáng shè

驕傲國，瞧不起高鐵車列。
jiāo ào guó　qiáo bú qǐ gāo tiě chē liè

變化不能測，帝國多不屑。
biàn huà bú néng cè　dì guó duō bú xiè

倦日撤，異鄉客。
juàn rì chè　yì xiāng kè

青夢不易舍，眷戀繽紛色。
qīng mèng bú yì shě　juàn liàn bīn fēn sè

秋風瑟，吹落漂零歸根葉。
qiū fēng sè　chuī luò piāo líng guī gēn yè

5.2 *Year of Thousand Autumns*

Autumn Day of Detroit

September 11, 2019

General Motors, Ford, and Chrysler,

Three role models of car manufacturer.

Living a suburban house, driving a Detroit car,

A middle-class haven and an American star.

Once an American dream,

Today's economic nightmare.

The proud country does not care,

What bullet trains like or where they are.

Changes are all over but empires not aware.

Living in a new land as a foreigner,

Dreams go on but not quite sure.

Autumn leaves fall to the familiar root area.

飛 行 常 客
fēi　xíng　cháng　kè

2019 年 10 月 11 日

機 場 空 中 ， 旅 途 本 痛 。
jī　chǎng　kōng　zhōng　　lǚ　tú　běn　tòng

閑 得 無 事 ， 樂 趣 全 空 。
xián　dé　wú　shì　　lè　qù　quán　kōng

寫 詩 填 詞 ， 磨 磨 時 鐘 。
xiě　shī　tián　cí　　mó　mó　shí　zhōng

稍 做 整 理 ， 分 享 與 眾 。
shāo　zuò　zhěng　lǐ　　fèn　xiǎng　yǔ　zhòng

多 思 時 快 ， 清 風 容 松 。
duō　sī　shí　kuài　　qīng　fēng　róng　sōng

抒 情 發 感 ， 其 樂 無 窮 。
shū　qíng　fā　gǎn　　qí　lè　wú　qióng

5.3　Frequent Flyer

October 11, 2019

At the airport or in the sky,

Travel itself is not for joy.

Not much to do when confined,

There is no glee but only void.

Compose and write,

Good way to kill time.

Structure it concise,

And share it wide.

Deep thinking makes time fly,

Like breeze relaxing eye.

Expressing ideas and feelings alike,

Harvest the joy during the flight.

聲　聲　慢
shēng　shēng　màn

疫　中　歸
yì　zhōng　guī

2020　年　3　月　13　日

零　零　落　落　，　　空　空　蕩　蕩　，
líng　líng　luò　luò　　　　kōng　kōng　dàng　dàng

陰　陰　沈　沈　唳　唳　。
yīn　yīn　chén　chén　lì　lì

欲　歸　還　恐　下　機　，
yù　guī　hái　kǒng　xià　jī

滿　目　蒼　夷　。
mǎn　mù　cāng　yí

走　時　仍　是　盛　世　，
zǒu　shí　réng　shì　shèng　shì

再　回　首　，　一　瀉　千　裏　。
zài　huí　shǒu　　　yī　xiè　qiān　lǐ

慎　距　離　，　人　自　危　。
shèn　jù　lí　　　rén　zì　wēi

空　乘　亦　擦　座　位　。
kōng　chéng　yì　cā　zuò　wèi

美國新冠狀疫情始發西雅圖。正逢差旅威斯康星州。遠聞西村疫情加重，風聲鶴唳。膽戰心驚回到家中。有感填此詞。

5.4.1 *Adagio of Tune by Tune*

Return Home in Epidemic

March 13, 2020

Scattered or empty,

Gloomy and scary.

Desperately want to go home,

Getting off the plane needs bravery.

All you see is dreary.

Good time was still in February,

Before the trip far away.

The downturn makes one weary.

Many are aware of distancing,

And actions deemed as risky.

Even the flight attendants,

Start to wipe seats for certainty.

The American COVID-19 pandemic initially started out in Seattle. I was traveling in Wisconsin. The situation suddenly got so serious that traveling to Seattle was considered too risky at that time. I decided to take the risk and flew back home.

5.4.2

聲　聲　慢
shēng　shēng　màn

疫　中　歸
yì　zhōng　guī

2020　年　3　月　13　日

疫　疾　不　分　我　你　，
yì　jí　bú　fèn　wǒ　nǐ

待　家　歸　，　妻　令　樓　下　隔　離　。
dài　jiā　guī　　qī　lìng　lóu　xià　gé　lí

獄　居　宅　室　，
yù　jū　zhái　shì

堪　稱　史　無　前　例　。
kān　chēng　shǐ　wú　qián　lì

冠　狀　天　下　無　敵　，
guàn　zhuàng　tiān　xià　wú　dí

西　村　雨　，　淅　淅　瀝　瀝　。
xī　cūn　yǔ　　xī　xī　lì　lì

這　次　第　，
zhè　cì　dì

惶　字　不　達　詞　義　。
huáng　zì　bú　dá　cí　yì

5.4.2 *Adagio of Tune by Tune*

Return Home in Epidemic

March 13, 2020

Virus is indifferent of you or me.

It gets wherever it can be.

Returning home from the place so dicey,

Immediately go to the quarantine misery.

Living in a room alone and lonely,

More like a prison detainee.

Imagine it spreads globally,

What an unprecedented catastrophe.

Virus still has no enemy.

Seattle's weather is so rainy.

The situation is dire and worsening.

Worrisome is not enough to express the feeling.

上線紀念
shàng xiàn jì niàn

2020 年 5 月 5 日

主　意　自　坊　間　，
zhǔ　yì　zì　fāng　jiān

系　統　終　上　線　。
xì　tǒng　zhōng　shàng　xiàn

不　知　成　多　少　，
bú　zhī　chéng　duō　shǎo

香　檳　是　時　間　。
xiāng　bīn　shì　shí　jiān

熱　鬧　喜　氣　添　，
rè　nào　xǐ　qì　tiān

缺　一　份　恬　然　。
quē　yī　fèn　tián　rán

填　首　雨　霖　鈴　，
tián　shǒu　yǔ　lín　líng

權　以　作　紀　念　。
quán　yǐ　zuò　jì　niàn

5.5　The Commemoration for Going Live

May 5, 2020

The idea comes from the public.

Final going live is historic.

Not sure how much it will bring,

Champagne time is for Sputnik.

Lively and joyful add up to ecstatic,

Mixing with peace would be perfect.

Write a poem of *The Bell Ringing in the Rain*,

Commemorating the extraordinary epic.

6 假　日
jiǎ　rì

HOLIDAYS

普　天　樂
pǔ　tiān　lè

美　國　勞　動　節
měi　guó　láo　dòng　jiē

2019　年　8　月　30　日

九　月　天　，　炊　煙　裊　。
jiǔ　yuè　tiān　　chuī　yān　niǎo

阿　米　麗　卡　，　夏　末　膾　烤　。
ā　mǐ　lì　kǎ　　xià　mò　kuài　kǎo

艷　陽　日　，　回　光　照　。
yàn　yáng　rì　　huí　guāng　zhào

中　意　盤　餐　數　漢　堡　，
zhōng　yì　pán　cān　shù　hàn　bǎo

米　勒　百　威　醉　不　倒　。
mǐ　lè　bǎi　wēi　zuì　bú　dǎo

年　復　一　年　，　比　基　尼　拋　，
nián　fù　yī　nián　　bǐ　jī　ní　pāo

又　送　君　走　。
yòu　sòng　jūn　zǒu

勞動節：九月第一個周一。在美國勞動節被認為是夏季的結束。

燒烤：勞動節第一活動　　　漢堡：勞動節第一盤中餐

啤酒：勞動節第一飲料。　　米勒百威：啤酒品牌 Miller, Budweiser

p6.1　*Worldwide Joy*

Labor Day of America

August 30, 2019

Smoke curls up from backyard,

In a fine day of September.

America enjoys the grill and bathing sun.

It is the last day of this Summer.

Bright sun ray is the predictor.

The favorite food has got to be the burger.

Won't make you drunk with Miller or Budweiser.

Toss the bikini for good year after year.

BBQ Grill: Number one activity for Labor Day. Burger: Number one food for Labor Day. Beer: Number one drink for Labor Day.

6.2　　　清　　江　　引
　　　　　qīng　jiāng　yǐn

感　恩　節
gǎn　ēn　jiē

2019　年　11　月　28　日

融　融　樂　樂　感　恩　節　，
róng　róng　lè　lè　gǎn　ēn　jiē

火　雞　愛　上　碟　。
huǒ　jī　ài　shàng　dié

親　人　洽　洽　聚　，
qīn　rén　qià　qià　jù

賢　婦　球　賽　瞥　。
xián　fù　qiú　sài　piē

媳　婿　兒　女　把　話　接　。
xí　xù　ér　nǚ　bǎ　huà　jiē

十一月最末周四，美國的感恩節。人們吃火雞，看橄欖球賽。年輕
人帶著伴侶回到父母家。這是合家團聚的日子，象中國的過年。

6.2　*Song of Clear River*

Thanksgiving Holiday

November 28, 2019

Happy and harmony display,

On the Thanksgiving holiday.

The favorite dish is on turkey plate.

Tradition itself is the cliche.

Preparing the feast for the day.

Taking a glimpse of the football play.

Mother and daughter, father and son,

Catch up with what each other say.

American Thanksgiving holiday is on the last Thursday of November. Traditionally people eat turkey meat and watch football. Young people bring their companions home. This is a time of family union, like the traditional Chinese New Year.

跨　年　二　〇　二　〇
kuà　nián　èr　líng　èr　líng

2019　年　12　月　31　日

千　年　如　昨　日　，
qiān　nián　rú　zuó　rì

回　首　乍　二　十　。
huí　shǒu　zhà　èr　shí

額　上　縷　冰　霜　，
é　shàng　lǚ　bīng　shuāng

不　是　天　冷　致　。
bú　shì　tiān　lěng　zhì

6.3　Ring in 2020

December 31, 2019

The millennium seems like yesterday,

Suddenly twenty years have slipped away.

Wisps of ice and frost turning the forehead grey.

It is not the weather that is making the tricky play.

憶　江　南
yì　jiāng　nán

過　年
guò　nián

2020　年　1　月　12　日

春　節　到　，
chūn　jié　dào

寒　梅　把　信　報　。
hán　méi　bǎ　xìn　bào

寰　宇　昂　首　東　方　翹　，
huán　yǔ　áng　shǒu　dōng　fāng　qiào

人　間　歡　樂　故　鄉　飄　。
rén　jiān　huān　lè　gù　xiāng　piāo

何　不　往　家　跑　？
hé　bú　wǎng　jiā　pǎo

6.4 *Memory of the Yangtze River South*

Celebrating Chinese New Year

January 12, 2020

The plum blossom has been telling,
The Spring is fast coming.
The Chinese New Year is the Spring Festival.
Nothing than that is more exciting.

The world raises its head to what's happening.
Pride of the East is up showing.
And the hometown glee is everywhere floating.
Why not ready and get home going?

重 疊 金
chóng dié jīn

疫 情 慶 新 年
yì qíng qìng xīn nián

2020 年 1 月 23 日

昨 周 西 村 瓢 大 雪 。
zuó zhōu xī cūn piáo dà xuě

同 樂 心 情 如 雀 躍 。
tóng lè xīn qíng rú què yuè

賦 短 短 新 詩 。
fù duǎn duǎn xīn shī

慶 融 融 除 夕 。
qìng róng róng chú xī

新 年 再 新 日 ，
xīn nián zài xīn rì

福 大 福 多 至 。
fú dà fú duō zhì

時 變 景 更 見 。
shí biàn jǐng gèng jiàn

仍 把 原 句 現 。
réng bǎ yuán jù xiàn

2020 年 1 月 12 日寫下《憶江南·過年》。不想新冠急轉直下，武漢同胞有家不能回。23 日感慨填《重疊金·西村新春》，再補《望江南·與你心同跳》。

6.5 *Pile of Money*

Celebrating New Year in Pandemic

January 23, 2020

The snow had been falling in Seattle since last week,

Happy mood stirred up by the snow-bird's beak.

Writing short poems for the New Year's Eve,

Let the heart and mind silently speak.

New year, new day and all things unique,

May many great blessings keep coming quick.

Time had changed and situation was different.

Still keep the joy to the cheek that we always seek.

I wrote the piece *"Reminiscing the Yangtze River South* - Celebrating the Chinese New Year" on January 12, 2020. Unexpectedly, the COVID-19 pandemic in Wuhan suddenly started deteriorating quickly. Folks could not go home for the Chinese New Year. This piece was written right before the Chinese New Year's Eve, along with another piece *"Overlooking the Yangtze River South* – We are With You with a Silent Prayer".

采　桑　子
cǎi　sāng　zǐ

聖　誕　快　樂
shèng　dàn　kuài　lè

2020　年　12　月　25　日

長　旅　他　鄉　隨　異　俗　。
cháng　lǚ　tā　xiāng　suí　yì　sú

倩　倩　西　圖　，
qiàn　qiàn　xī　tú

漸　心　安　處　。
jiàn　xīn　ān　chù

居　久　亦　成　二　故　土　。
jū　jiǔ　yì　chéng　èr　gù　tǔ

上　帝　賜　福　聖　誕　祝　。
shàng　dì　cì　fú　shèng　dàn　zhù

親　朋　鄰　居　，
qīn　péng　lín　jū

天　涯　山　麓　。
tiān　yá　shān　lù

青　春　如　初　樂　永　駐　。
qīng　chūn　rú　chū　lè　yǒng　zhù

6.6 *Mulberry Picking*

Merry Christmas

December 25, 2020

Travel of a long duration in a foreign land,

Imperative to adapt life to different customs demand.

Living in attractive Seattle like typical American.

Gradually feel at ease and slowly understand.

It becomes second hometown after a long-time span.

The home sports team is the homeland to defend.

"Christmas is coming" sings the parade music band.

Join the crowd to celebrate wherever you can.

God gives us blessings with his mighty hand.

Relative, neighbor or my friend,

Far away over the horizon or long-range mountain,

May happiness be with you and youth forever stand.

浣 溪 沙
huàn　xī　shā

牛 年
niú　nián

2021 年 2 月 11 日

月虧過後得月盈，
yuè kuī guò hòu dé yuè yíng

破舊除廢才立新，
pò jiù chú fèi cái lì xīn

鼠輩眾裏顯牛人。
shǔ bèi zhòng lǐ xiǎn niú rén

酷寒嚴冬珍梅馨，
kù hán yán dōng zhēn méi xīn

驅鼠去穢霸方今，
qū shǔ qù huì bà fāng jīn

順心自然想事成。
shùn xīn zì rán xiǎng shì chéng

牛氣沖天的股市，希望帶來新年的好運。

6.7　*Sand Beach of Silk Washing Stream*

The Year of Ox

February 11, 2021

The full moon comes after the crescent.

Letting go of the old keeps the new incessant.

The mediocre sets apart the excellent.

Bitter cold winter makes plum blossom radiant.

Replacing Rat with Ox, the year will be abundant.

Following self-nature, the success will be present.

May the early signs of the strong bullish stock market bring in the good luck for the Chinese New Year.

蔔　算　子
bǔ　　suàn　　zǐ

清　明
qīng　　míng

2021　年　4　月　5　日

親　是　新　黃　花　，
qīn　shì　xīn　huáng　huā

甜　是　去　年　橘　。
tián　shì　qù　nián　jú

哪　邊　易　尋　家　鄉　水　，
nǎ　biān　yì　xún　jiā　xiāng　shuǐ

眉　眼　盈　盈　處　。
méi　yǎn　yíng　yíng　chù

西　村　無　清　明　，
xī　cūn　wú　qīng　míng

異　鄉　久　亦　故　。
yì　xiāng　jiǔ　yì　gù

春　風　若　是　通　仙　靈　，
chūn　fēng　ruò　shì　tōng　xiān　líng

捎　話　與　祖　母　。
shāo　huà　yǔ　zǔ　mǔ

油菜花是新溪的地方花。橘子是主要地方水果。

6.8 *Divination Minor*

The Pure Brightness Festival

April 5, 2021

It feels like family to see the yellow flower.

It melts the heart to eat the orange of last year.

Look no harder than below the eyebrow,

That is where to easily find hometown water.

The Pure Brightness is for respecting past ancestor.

Second hometown Seattle does not have such a culture.

If only the wind of Spring connects to the heaven,

Please help relay the message to my grandmother.

The yellow canola flower is the town flower for Xinxi. The orange is the primary fruit in the town.

6.9　　最　真　天　下　慈　母　心　　　　45
　　　　zuì　zhēn　tiān　xià　cí　mǔ　xīn

2019　年　5　月　9　日

最　親　親　人　是　娘　親　，
zuì　qīn　qīn　rén　shì　niáng　qīn

最　真　真　情　母　最　真　，
zuì　zhēn　zhēn　qíng　mǔ　zuì　zhēn

異　鄉　遊　子　繈　褓　兒　，
yì　xiāng　yóu　zǐ　qiǎng　bǎo　ér

莫　不　牽　掛　慈　母　心　。
mò　bú　qiān　guà　cí　mǔ　xīn

母親節是五月的第二個星期日。二〇二一年的母親節是五月九日。

6.9　The Truest is a Mother's Heart

May 9, 2021

The closest family is the dear mother.

The truest love is forever from her.

Whether an infant or a foreign land wanderer,

It is the loving mother's heart that provides the shelter.

Mother's Day is on the second Sunday of May. It is on May 9 for 2021.

一　剪　梅
yī　　jiǎn　　méi

中　秋
zhōng　　qiū

2021　年　9　月　21　日

憶　昔　中　秋　玉　掛　高　，
yì　xī　zhōng　qiū　yù　guà　gāo

小　平　您　好　，　北　京　年　少　。
xiǎo　píng　nín　hǎo　　běi　jīng　nián　shǎo

更　有　童　時　江　南　曉　，
gèng　yǒu　tóng　shí　jiāng　nán　xiǎo

山　也　清　秀　，　人　也　清　秀　。
shān　yě　qīng　xiù　　rén　yě　qīng　xiù

待　邁　美　洲　開　普　角　，
dài　mài　měi　zhōu　kāi　pǔ　jiǎo

苦　也　劍　橋　，　樂　也　劍　橋　。
kǔ　yě　jiàn　qiáo　　lè　yě　jiàn　qiáo

而　今　西　村　皓　月　照　，
ér　jīn　xī　cūn　hào　yuè　zhào

山　水　依　舊　，　聊　永　今　朝　。
shān　shuǐ　yī　jiù　　liáo　yǒng　jīn　zhāo

6.10 *Twig of Plum Blossom*

Middle Autumn

September 21, 2021

It's like yesternight in Beijing,

With a giant jade plate up high hanging.

"Hello, Xiaoping",

Young China just started opening.

Still remember the River South Mountain,

The water was crystal clean,

The handsome and beautiful people,

And ever childhood Yangtze River morning.

Until seeing the Cape Code scene,

The immense experience of American schooling.

Bitter in Cambridge, happy in Cambridge,

The whole new world for exploring.

Seattle's water is as blue as trees are green,

With the full moon up and shining,

Thirty years of Mid-Autumn do not change much a thing.

Forever we care about the present with more talking.

cháng mìng nǔ

感恩季

gǎn ēn jì

2021 年 11 月 25 日

感 恩 季 ，
gǎn ēn jì

火 雞 一 只 酒 一 杯 ，
huǒ jī yī zhī jiǔ yī bēi

謝 恩 有 三 記 。
xiè ēn yǒu sān jì

一 記 上 蒼 美 意 ，
yī jì shàng cāng měi yì

二 記 團 圓 福 至 ，
èr jì tuán yuán fú zhì

三 記 豐 收 盈 滿 溢 。
sān jì fēng shōu yíng mǎn yì

年 年 好 節 期 。
nián nián hǎo jiē qī

感恩節，美國法定節日。家家團圓，戶戶感恩。開始了一年一度的
感恩、聖誕、新年的假日季節。

6.11 *Lady of Longevity*

The Season of Thanksgiving

November 25, 2021

On the Thanksgiving Day,

A turkey on the tray,

With a glass of wine,

Three grateful things to say.

The god's blessing when pray,

The family reunion when away,

And the harvest and abundance,

Won't be able to repay.

Year over year on the way,

Good days come in an array.

To wish all good and well,

And another wonderful holiday.

Thanksgiving is America's official holiday. Families have reunions. Household give thanks. Thanksgiving kicks off a season of holidays for Thanksgiving, Christmas and New Year.

7 外　遊
wài　yóu

TRAVEL

八　聲　甘　州
bā　shēng　gān　zhōu

登　高　七　月　四　日
dēng　gāo　qī　yuè　sì　rì

2019　年　7　月　4　日

獨　立　日　、　布　兵　林　肯　堂　，
dú　lì　rì　　bù　bīng　lín　kěn　táng

三　軍　寫　臉　上　。
sān　jūn　xiě　liǎn　shàng

海　軍　陸　戰　隊　，
hǎi　jūn　lù　zhàn　duì

陸　軍　坦　克　，　空　軍　機　響　。
lù　jūn　tǎn　kè　　kōng　jūn　jī　xiǎng

帝　國　史　無　前　例　，
dì　guó　shǐ　wú　qián　lì

似　閱　兵　紅　場　。
sì　yuè　bīng　hóng　chǎng

昂　首　美　利　堅　，　誰　學　他　樣　？
áng　shǒu　měi　lì　jiān　　shuí　xué　tā　yàng

7　外　遊　TRAVEL

7.1.1　*Eight Tunes of Ganzhou*

Hiking on the 4th of July

July 4, 2019

On the Independence Day,
At Lincoln Memorial to display,
Three branches of military,
In an unprecedented parade.

Marines from Navy,
Tanks from Army,
And the bombers that are stealthy,
All zooming in Washington D.C.

History will have a say,
The Red-Square like child play,
The arrogant American way,
All will make America pay.

7.1.2

八　聲　甘　州
bā　shēng　gān　zhōu

登　高　七　月　四　日
dēng　gāo　qī　yuè　sì　rì

2019　年　7　月　4　日

夏　日　氣　爽　登　高　，
xià　rì　qì　shuǎng　dēng　gāo

四　山　只　一　趟　，　漫　遊　徜　徉　。
sì　shān　zhī　yī　tàng　　màn　yóu　cháng　yáng

山　低　路　遠　長　，
shān　dī　lù　yuǎn　cháng

個　人　紀　錄　榜　。
gè　rén　jì　lù　bǎng

想　當　年　、　二　國　集　團　，
xiǎng　dāng　nián　　èr　guó　jí　tuán

看　今　日　、　恐　塵　封　泡　湯　。
kàn　jīn　rì　　kǒng　chén　fēng　pào　tāng

只　可　惜　，　阿　米　麗　卡　，
zhī　kě　xī　　ā　mǐ　lì　kǎ

無　人　治　恙　。
wú　rén　zhì　yàng

四山： Somerset, Hilltop, Summit, Cougar Mountain

個人紀錄：日登山 16.5 邁，26.4 公裏。

二國集團： G2 of ChinAmerica

122

7.1.2　*Eight Tunes of Ganzhou*

Hiking on the 4th of July

July 4, 2019

Beautiful Seattle Summer ray,

Not different from that in the month of May,

Hiking four mountains in one way,

You are in your prime when in your heyday.

The mountains are low but it's a long way,

With a personal record to gasconade.

The Group of Two from Obama day,

No longer in play however you look at it today.

The American dream will stay,

Regardless of what people claim.

Only if someone stands up and yell nay,

Put it back to the right trajectory.

Four Mountains: Somerset, Hilltop, Summit, Cougar Mountain

Personal Record: Daily hiking of 16.5 miles, 26.4 kilometers

G2: Group of Two - ChinAmerica

二 登 颶 風 峰

èr　dēng　jù　fēng　fēng

2019　年　8　月　9　日

昔　登　奧　林　匹　克　山　，
xī　dēng　ào　lín　pǐ　kè　shān

大　霧　彌　漫　雲　遮　天　。
dà　wù　mí　màn　yún　zhē　tiān

待　到　雲　開　霧　散　日　，
dài　dào　yún　kāi　wù　sàn　rì

方　知　原　到　世　之　巔　。
fāng　zhī　yuán　dào　shì　zhī　diān

颶風峰：位於美國華盛頓州奧林匹克國家公園。

7.2　Revisit the Hurricane Ridge

August 9, 2019

When first visiting the Olympic Mountain site,

It was a cloudy day with everything in white.

Until this time when it's sunny and bright,

Then realize we were at the top of the world,
only without sight.

The Hurricane Ridge is located in the Olympic National Park, State of Washington, U.S.A.

西　岸　東　岸
xī　àn　dōng　àn

2019　年　8　月　10　日

昔　怨　發　貼　朋　友　圈　，
xī　yuàn　fā　tiē　péng　yǒu　quān

逢　假　多　往　附　近　轉　。
féng　jiǎ　duō　wǎng　fù　jìn　zhuǎn

西　圖　本　就　天　堂　般　，
xī　tú　běn　jiù　tiān　táng　bān

何　要　舍　近　而　求　遠　？
hé　yào　shě　jìn　ér　qiú　yuǎn

天　使　港　灣　左　右　看　，
tiān　shǐ　gǎng　wān　zuǒ　yòu　kàn

喜　見　遊　人　兩　國　穿　。
xǐ　jiàn　yóu　rén　liǎng　guó　chuān

一　○　一　路　並　不　寬　，
yī　líng　yī　lù　bìng　bú　kuān

最　美　風　景　往　南　觀　。
zuì　měi　fēng　jǐng　wǎng　nán　guān

天使港灣: Port of Angeles，華盛頓州西北，毗鄰加拿大維多利亞。

一○一: 美國 101 公路

7.3.1　West Coast and East Coast

August 10, 2019

Wife whining in a posting to a friend circle,
Vacationing too often too close to home.
The summer of heaven is in Seattle,
Why would you bother to venture off local?

Look at the busy cross-border terminal,
In and out you see happy people hustle.
Route 101 does not much bustle.
The best scenery is in the south and coastal.

7.3.2

西 岸 東 岸
xī àn dōng àn

2019 年 8 月 10 日

天 若 有 心 聽 我 喚 ，
tiān ruò yǒu xīn tīng wǒ huàn

太 平 洋 變 小 河 川 。
tài píng yáng biàn xiǎo hé chuān

助 我 扔 石 到 彼 岸 ，
zhù wǒ rēng shí dào bǐ àn

更 勝 網 上 音 訊 傳 。
gèng shèng wǎng shàng yīn xùn chuán

美 洲 大 陸 應 西 端 ，
měi zhōu dà lù yīng xī duān

太 平 洋 上 該 東 灣 。
tài píng yáng shàng gāi dōng wān

西 岸 東 岸 如 何 算 ？
xī àn dōng àn rú hé suàn

南 來 北 往 靠 大 宣 。
nán lái běi wǎng kào dà xuān

7.3.2　West Coast and East Coast

August 10, 2019

If only God responds to my sincere appeal,

The Pacific would become a narrow channel.

Then I will pick a small rock and just throw,

Easier to send a message to the old hometown than email.

Seattle is on the west coast is factual.

Saying it's on the east coast of the Pacific is a hard sale.

West Coast or East Coast, how can you really tell?

The one who has less discourse power will always fail.

7.4.1

三　登　樂
sān　dēng　lè

雨　林　漫　霧
yǔ　lín　màn　wù

2019　年　8　月　11　日

雨　林　漫　霧　，
yǔ　lín　màn　wù

天　使　港　，　煩　惱　皆　除　。
tiān　shǐ　gǎng　　fán　nǎo　jiē　chú

月　亮　湖　，　水　清　若　無　。
yuè　liàng　hú　　shuǐ　qīng　ruò　wú

雨　如　絲　，　溫　泉　綠　，
yǔ　rú　sī　　wēn　quán　lù

池　潤　肌　膚　。
chí　rùn　jī　fū

青　苔　如　柳　，
qīng　tái　rú　liǔ

樹　像　天　柱　。
shù　xiàng　tiān　zhù

7.4.1 *Joy of Twenty-Seven Years of Good Harvest*

Meandering Fog in the Rain Forest

August 11, 2019

In the fresh warm rain forest,

The American's Northwest,

Floating, flying and meandering mist,

Puts all worries and troubles to rest.

In the crystal-clear Lake Crescent,

The water is the cleanest.

Port Angeles, and the nearest,

The paradise you will never forget.

Rain like silk, the hot spring is verdant,

Moisturizing skin with the finest.

Moss like willows, the trees are splendid.

The enchantment forest is magnificent.

7.4.2 三　　登　　樂
　　　　sān　　dēng　　lè

雨　　林　　漫　　霧
yǔ　　lín　　màn　　wù

2019　年　8　月　11　日

天　　際　　遠　、　一　　線　　粗　，
tiān　jì　　yuǎn　　yī　　xiàn　cū

海　　出　　新　　物　。
hǎi　chū　xīn　　wù

夕　　陽　　紅　、　且　　當　　日　　出　。
xī　　yáng　hóng　　qiě　dāng　rì　　chū

少　　年　　心　、　願　　如　　初　，
shǎo　nián　xīn　　yuàn　rú　　chū

殷　　殷　　期　　許　。
yīn　yīn　qī　　xǔ

依　　依　　不　　舍　，
yī　　yī　　bú　　shě

留　　戀　　卻　　步　。
liú　liàn　què　bù

7.4.2 *Joy of Twenty-Seven Years of Good Harvest*

Meandering Fog in the Rain Forest

August 11, 2019

With the horizon out the farthest,

In a line of the thinnest,

Ocean and sky meet,

Beautiful things are all at the feet.

From afar the smallest,

To the things at the closest,

Emerging out of the sea at the sunset.

Isn't the wonderful time to come yet?

A young and innocent heart,

With wishes right at the start,

Sunset is red, reluctant to part.

Nature with people is beautiful art.

山　外　有　山
shān　wài　yǒu　shān

2019　年　8　月　24　日

西　村　信　箱　山 ，
xī　cūn　xìn　xiāng　shān

陡　不　易　攀 。
dǒu　bú　yì　pān

堪　如　登　蜀　道 ，
kān　rú　dēng　shǔ　dào

難　於　上　天 。
nán　yú　shàng　tiān

今　登　布　蘭　卡 ，
jīn　dēng　bù　lán　kǎ

頂　峰　過　冰　川 。
dǐng　fēng　guò　bīng　chuān

長　噓　嘆 、　山　外　有　山 。
cháng　xū　tàn　　shān　wài　yǒu　shān

信箱山：Mailbox Peak，海拔 4822 英尺，登峰來回 9.4 英裏，西雅圖往東半小時車程。布蘭卡湖：Blanca Lake，湖海拔 3300 英尺，爬峰海拔 4600 英尺，來回 11.5 英裏，西雅圖東北二小時車程。西雅圖：海拔 0 英尺（海港就在城中心）

7.5.1 *Cool Breeze of Orchid*

There is Another Mountain Over a Mountain

August 24, 2019

The steep mailbox mountain peak,

Easy to make hikers freak,

As hard as the ancient road made of plank,

Going upward is an impossible task.

Today's hiking to Blanca Lake,

Up and down lets muscle ache.

One by one I'm counting,

There is another mountain over a mountain.

Mailbox Peak: Elevation of 4,822 feet, hiking round trip of 9.4 miles, half hour of driving from Seattle. Blanc Lake: Elevation of 3,300 feet, Mountain Peak elevation of 4,600 feet, hiking round trip of 11.5 miles, two hours of driving from Seattle.

7.5.2　　　　蕙　　清　　風
　　　　　　huì　　qīng　　fēng

山　外　有　山
shān　wài　yǒu　shān

2019　年　8　月　24　日

上　　下　　來　　回　　翻　，
shàng　xià　　lái　　huí　　fān

極　　不　　平　　坦　。
jí　　bú　　píng　　tǎn

越　　嶺　　如　　長　　征　，
yuè　　lǐng　　rú　　cháng　zhēng

意　　不　　再　　返　。
yì　　bú　　zài　　fǎn

遇　　古　　稀　　老　　漢　，
yù　　gǔ　　xī　　lǎo　　hàn

心　　頓　　感　　汗　　顏　。
xīn　　dùn　　gǎn　　hàn　　yán

人　　世　　間　、　能　　人　　能　　幹　。
rén　　shì　　jiān　　　néng　rén　néng　gàn

7.5.2　*Cool Breeze of Orchid*

There is Another Mountain Over a Mountain

August 24, 2019

Summit and glacier, forward and back,
Extremely uneven and winding like snake.
Crossing the mountain tops like the Long March trek,
Coming back for another trip would be a big mistake.

On the way back met an elderly bloke.
His pace was slow but without any shake.
Suddenly felt ashamed for the age's sake.
There is extraordinary when ordinary would break.

水　調　歌　頭
shuǐ　diào　gē　tóu

夏　日　冰　島
xià　rì　bīng　dǎo

2019　年　12　月　21　日

坐　中　大　西　洋　，
zuò　zhōng　dà　xī　yáng

臨　近　北　極　光　。
lín　jìn　běi　jí　guāng

太　陽　倦　慵　怠　工　，
tài　yáng　juàn　yōng　dài　gōng

日　出　日　落　忘　。
rì　chū　rì　luò　wàng

到　處　山　青　水　茫　，
dào　chù　shān　qīng　shuǐ　máng

恰　似　江　南　柳　塘　。
qià　sì　jiāng　nán　liǔ　táng

大　巴　中　國　腔　。
dà　bā　zhōng　guó　qiāng

瀑　布　半　天　上　，
bào　bù　bàn　tiān　shàng

黑　灘　引　人　往　。
hēi　tān　yǐn　rén　wǎng

西雅圖的黑夜今天最長，往後的白晝只會越來越長。夏天也越來越近。去年的冰島遊仿佛是昨天。

7.6.1 *Prelude to the Water Melody*

Summer in Iceland

December 21, 2019

Halfway in the Northern Atlantic,
Close to the Northern Lights of the Arctic,
A European oasis outside of Europe,
Iceland is uniquely majestic.

Summer sun is soft and laid back,
Forgetting sunrise and sunset.
Green hills and waters are vast,
Reminding the willow pond of the past.

Shuttle tour bus with Chinese accent,
Waterfall from the sky high falling fast,
Black sand beach has no limit,
People from all over the world love to visit.

7.6.2

水 調 歌 頭
shuǐ diào gē tóu

夏 日 冰 島
xià rì bīng dǎo

2019 年 12 月 21 日

居 北 方 ， 海 水 涼 ，
jū běi fāng hǎi shuǐ liáng

不 能 蹚 。
bú néng tāng

待 泡 藍 色 泉 湯 ，
dài pào lán sè quán tāng

如 浸 滑 泥 漿 。
rú jìn huá ní jiāng

難 得 世 間 別 樣 ，
nán dé shì jiān bié yàng

只 能 親 身 試 嘗 。
zhī néng qīn shēn shì cháng

帶 著 青 夢 想 。
dài zhe qīng mèng xiǎng

只 要 不 崇 洋 ，
zhī yào bú chóng yáng

月 兒 也 更 亮 。
yuè ér yě gèng liàng

140

7.6.2 *Prelude to the Water Melody*

Summer in Iceland

December 21, 2019

Situated in northern high latitude,

Cold sea water is very frigid.

Wading water is not recommended,

The risk is of enormous magnitude.

Immersing into the hot spring pool,

The slip mud feeling is so cool.

Blue sky, blue sea and the pool is blue too.

Only experiencing it realizes it is true.

It is great to have a dream,

As long as maintaining the self-esteem.

The moonlight may have different gleam,

Not because it is supreme.

2020　年　12　月　24　日

天　涯　走　，　　域　外　遊　，
tiān　yá　zǒu　　　yù　wài　yóu

識　多　廣　，　　樂　悠　悠　。
shí　duō　guǎng　　lè　yōu　yōu

有　對　照　，　　才　比　較　，
yǒu　duì　zhào　　cái　bǐ　jiào

山　外　山　，　　樓　外　樓　。
shān　wài　shān　　lóu　wài　lóu

逆　水　舟　，　　見　劣　優　，
nì　shuǐ　zhōu　　jiàn　liè　yōu

追　四　方　，　　上　下　求　。
zhuī　sì　fāng　　shàng　xià　qiú

7.7.1   Off to See the World

December 24, 2020

Visiting faraway world,

Travel to land abroad.

Knowing more and wide,

Enjoy a slow joy ride.

Only with differentiation,

Can you do a comparison.

There is mountain over mountain,

There is building across building.

Sailing against the current,

Know the good and the deficient.

Exploring not only the apparent,

Chase up and down and be diligent.

7.7.2 域　外　遊
　　　yù　　wài　　yóu

2020 年 12 月 24 日

思　不　周　，　莫　犯　愁　，
sī　bú　zhōu　　mò　fàn　chóu

不　局　格　，　竟　自　由　。
bú　jú　gé　　jìng　zì　yóu

知　多　少　，　創　意　謀　，
zhī　duō　shǎo　　chuàngyì　móu

出　匣　子　，　幄　運　籌　。
chū　xiá　zǐ　　wò　yùn　chóu

心　寬　厚　，　人　長　久　，
xīn　kuān　hòu　　rén　cháng　jiǔ

似　金　秋　，　大　豐　收　。
sì　jīn　qiū　　dà　fēng　shōu

7.7.2　Off to See the World

December 24, 2020

Not thinking through,

Don't worry much ado.

Not bounded by rule,

Strive to be free and cool.

Regardless of knowledge span,

Remain creative to strategic plan,

Stay out of confined den,

Command military with a pen.

With a generous heart,

Live a long life smart.

Like a golden Autumn cart,

Happy to have a bumper harvest.

點絳唇

diǎn jiàng chún

登 二 十 二 號 湖
dēng èr shí èr hào hú

2020 年 12 月 27 日

層 巒 西 圖 ，
céng luán xī tú

卡 斯 卡 底 擋 東 路 。
kǎ sī kǎ dǐ dǎng dōng lù

南 來 北 去 ，
nán lái běi qù

跨 北 美 西 部 。
kuà běi měi xī bù

太 平 洋 岸 ，
tài píng yáng àn

世 界 橫 斷 處 。
shì jiè héng duàn chù

峰 如 簇 ， 高 山 湖 舉 ，
fēng rú cù   gāo shān hú jǔ

引 多 少 逐 鹿 。
yǐn duō shǎo zhú lù

7.8 *Embellishing the Crimson Lips*

Hiking Lake 22
December 27, 2020

Mountains over mountains to reach Seattle,

The Cascade blocks the east bound road.

From North to South the ranges flow,

Start in Canada and end in Mexico.

On the east side of the Pacific Rim,

The picture of the fault line is grim.

Many explorers and amateur hikers,

Pursue to conquer mountain lake's brim.

玉　樓　春
yù　lóu　chūn

登　雷　涅　雪　山
dēng　léi　niè　xuě　shān

2021　年　1　月　3　日

三　英　裏　高　雷　涅　山　，
sān　yīng　lǐ　gāo　léi　niè　shān

三　百　米　深　普　吉　灣　。
sān　bǎi　mǐ　shēn　pǔ　jí　wān

山　下　細　煙　雨　蒙　蒙　，
shān　xià　xì　yān　yǔ　méng　méng

山　上　冰　花　雪　紛　紛　。
shān　shàng　bīng　huā　xuě　fēn　fēn

西　村　城　外　翠　森　森　，
xī　cūn　chéng　wài　cuì　sēn　sēn

青　杉　綠　柏　最　易　尋　。
qīng　shān　lù　bǎi　zuì　yì　xún

聖　誕　元　旦　節　已　過　，
shèng　dàn　yuán　dàn　jiē　yǐ　guò

期　盼　寒　梅　早　報　春　。
qī　pàn　hán　méi　zǎo　bào　chūn

7.9 *Spring of the Jade Tower*

Hiking Mount Rainier

January 3, 2021

Three-mile-high Rainier has the record to keep.

Puget Sound is three hundred meters deep.

The lowland sees the rain drip by drip.

Going to the mountain needs snow chain jeep.

Outside Seattle all look green,

Cedar and cypress make up the scene.

With Christmas and New Year already passing,

Look forward to plum blossom heralding Spring.

高 山 流 水
gāo shān liú shuǐ

大 峽 谷
dà xiá gǔ

2021 年 9 月 14 日

五 千 萬 年 細 功 夫 ，
wǔ qiān wàn nián xì gōng fū

三 裏 深 、 高 原 低 峪 。
sān lǐ shēn gāo yuán dī yù

滴 滴 穿 石 水 ，
dī dī chuān shí shuǐ

不 見 長 闊 平 湖 。
bú jiàn cháng kuò píng hú

近 閉 眼 、 為 第 一 目 。
jìn bì yǎn wéi dì yī mù

年 輪 數 ， 加 州 參 天 紅 杉 ，
nián lún shù jiā zhōu cān tiān hóng shān

相 形 見 絀 。
xiàng xíng jiàn chù

地 質 天 文 尺 ，
dì zhì tiān wén chǐ

一 切 皆 不 足 。
yī qiē jiē bú zú

7.10.1 *High Mountain and Flowing Water*

The Grand Canyon

September 14, 2021

Fifty million years of relentless hard work,

Plateau turning into valley with three miles deep effort.

Every drop of the stone piercing water,

Gone with a long and wide plateau lake forever.

Close the eyes when getting close,

Only to get the first sight shocking experience.

The California towering Sequoia trees,

Cannot even hold a candle to the canyon's breeze.

Measuring time uses the hour.

Gauging distance applies the yard.

When the Grand Canyon needs a ruler,

Anything in world is an insufficient meter.

7.10.2

高　山　流　水
gāo　shān　liú　shuǐ

大　峽　谷
dà　xiá　gǔ

2021　年　9　月　14　日

勿　語　。
wù　yǔ

冰　河　創　奇　跡　，
bīng　hé　chuàng　qí　jì

奪　天　工　、　造　化　神　術　。
duó　tiān　gōng　zào　huà　shén　shù

一　寸　一　千　年　，
yǐ　cùn　yǐ　qiān　nián

鐵　杵　磨　針　亦　算　輸　。
tiě　chǔ　mó　zhēn　yì　suàn　shū

光　陰　速　，　人　生　百　年　，
guāng　yīn　sù　rén　shēng　bǎi　nián

太　易　虛　度　。
tài　yì　xū　dù

日　復　日　相　顧　，
rì　fù　rì　xiàng　gù

千　載　論　峽　谷　。
qiān　zǎi　lùn　xiá　gǔ

7.10.2 *High Mountain and Flowing Water*

The Grand Canyon

September 14, 2021

Awed and speechless.

The glacier is miraculous.

Heavenly work no lacking genius,

The divine art of creation is fabulous.

One inch in a thousand year,

Anyone daring to compare is a loser.

The speed of humankind,

Only a hundred years of lifetime.

Life is too short we all do know,

We need to live it and live it well.

The Grand Canyon has a story to tell,

A millennium is only a short while.

8 異 域 文 化
yì　　yù　　wén　　huà

FOREIGN CULTURE

本非鐘愛海灘之人，眾雲隨波，始遊夏威夷。商業化之"盧奧"宴會，偶被選為觀眾示範，獲"皇家待遇"。後覺價非所值。頗感惆悵落失。

燈火闌珊之處，一不顯眼矮小歌臺。悠閑觀"呼拉"舞。見一窈窕舞女，金髮碧眼，婀娜多姿。呼拉波濤，忽左忽右，又上又下，欲動還靜。直看不像混血人，卻有東方之韻。樂之所至，情之所及，令人流連忘返。太平洋中，微小島嶼，不乏現代人間所有，然則遠離人間，堪為世外桃源。

8.1.1　New Tale of the Peach Blossom Land

Not quite a beach lover, I am the kind to go with the flow and follow with the crowd and began to visit Hawaii. We were selected as the audience demonstration and won the "Royal Courtesy" for the highly commercialized Luau banquet. Afterwards I fell in kind of gloomy mood for the unworthy price.

While wondering leisurely in the exotic scenery, in a place where the lights were dim, there was an inconspicuous small singing platform. The Hula Dance was on display. On the platform was a graceful dancer with blond hair and blue eyes. The Hula waves, were just like water, left and right, up and down, with sudden moves or instantly still. The Hula girl did not seem mixed race but had the charm of the East. Where the music came, where the smile went. It made people linger and forget to leave. On the small islands in the Pacific Ocean, there are all kinds of luxurious things that the modern world would provide. The islands are far away from the ordinary world and are regarded as paradise, similar to the "Peach Blossom Land" back 1,600 years in Chinese history.

8.1.2　新桃花源記

又過數年，欣然歸往，尋向所記，呼拉舞女，不復得之。後遂友自西村，聞之驚奇，年年往返，屢屢蒞臨，欲探究竟。終未果。惟有海天一色，白沙長灘依舊。今次西村陽光燦爛，似是帶回洋中沙灘。甚是感喟。故作此文此詩。

2021 年 6 月 19 日

8.1.2　　　New Tale of the Peach Blossom Land

After a few years, we happily returned to Hawaii, trying to find what we saw before. The Hula dancer was nowhere to be found. Later, friends from Seattle were surprised to hear the story with enormous curiosity. They went back year after year and came to explore it again and again. They never eventually had any success. Only the sea and sky are of the same color, and the white sand beach remains the way it used to be. Today Seattle is sunny, which seems to bring all back to the sand beach in the middle of the ocean. It is incredibly amazing. With the feeling I have, I decided to write this essay and the poem "Jade Butterfly – The Wave Beauty of Sea and Sky".

June 19, 2021

8.2.1

玉　蝴　蝶
yù　hú　dié

凌　波　海　天
líng　bō　hǎi　tiān

2021　年　6　月　19　日

白　沙　長　灘　如　練　，
bái　shā　cháng　tān　rú　liàn

柳　腰　梨　臀　，　凌　波　海　天　。
liǔ　yāo　lí　tún　　líng　bō　hǎi　tiān

冰　肌　玉　膚　，
bīng　jī　yù　fū

黛　眉　明　眸　桃　面　。
dài　méi　míng　móu　táo　miàn

姣　嬌　見　、　似　水　柔　情　，
jiāo　jiāo　jiàn　sì　shuǐ　róu　qíng

芳　步　輕　、　霓　裳　夭　艷　。
fāng　bù　qīng　ní　shang　yāo　yàn

瑤　池　邊　。
yáo　chí　biān

漫　飛　綃　雲　，　飄　忽　天　仙　。
màn　fēi　xiāo　yún　　piāo　hū　tiān　xiān

8.2.1　*Jade Butterfly*

The Wave Beauty of Sky and Sea

June 19, 2021

The wave beauty of sky and sea,

Like a pear and willow fairy.

Mingling with water and mountain,

The long sand beach is just as silky.

Bright eyes glittering,

Rosy cheeks shining.

With the posture heart melting,

It's every way that is dazzling.

Beautiful and tender, blue and white,

The steps and the cloths, light, and bright.

By the Jade Lake of the heavenly height,

The gauze clouds are flying not blocking sight.

8.2.2　　玉　蝴　蝶
　　　　　yù　　hú　　dié

凌　波　海　天
líng　bō　hǎi　tiān

2021 年 6 月 19 日

常　念　孔　雀　之　屏　，
cháng niàn kǒng què zhī píng

白　鶴　之　頸　，　乍　動　還　恬　。
bái　hè　zhī　jǐng　　zhà dòng hái tián

欲　滴　青　春　，
yù　dī　qīng　chūn

恰　豐　韻　朝　氣　四　綻　。
qià fēng yùn cháo qì sì zhàn

待　回　首　、　風　情　萬　種　，
dài huí shǒu　　fēng qíng wàn zhǒng

莫　多　言　、　遐　想　萬　千　。
mò duō yán　　xiá xiǎng wàn qiān

盡　醉　眼　。
jìn zuì yǎn

不　可　擾　夢　，　流　水　華　年　。
bú　kě　rǎo　mèng　　liú shuǐ huá nián

8.2.2 *Jade Butterfly*

The Wave Beauty of Sky and Sea

June 19, 2021

Often heard about peacocking fanning its tail,
Crane moving its legs with ballet skill.
The overflowing youth vibrance,
Displaying in an extraordinary scale.

Charm and charisma,
Glamour and vigor,
Vitality and fascination,
Only in unlimited imagination.

Eyes would get drunk.
Let dream not get sunk.
Think out of the confined trunk,
The wonderful years would easily do a bunk.

清　平　樂
qīng　　píng　　yuè

詠　冠　軍　多　倫　多
yǒng　guàn　jūn　duō　lún　duō

2019　年　6　月　13　日

北　方　的　狼　。
běi　fāng　de　láng

稱　霸　本　五　場　。
chēng　bà　běn　wǔ　chǎng

一　分　之　差　六　賽　長　。
yī　fèn　zhī　chà　liù　sài　cháng

看　似　五　場　重　放　。
kàn　sì　wǔ　chǎng　chóng　fàng

加　國　猛　禽　驚　慌　。
jiā　guó　měng　qín　jīng　huāng

金　州　王　朝　重　傷　。
jīn　zhōu　wáng　cháo　zhòng　shāng

驚　心　最　後　一　秒　，
jīng　xīn　zuì　hòu　yī　miǎo

中　外　同　贏　是　王　。
zhōng　wài　tóng　yíng　shì　wáng

全美籃協（NBA）二〇一九年決賽前五場比分（多倫多猛禽:金州勇士）- 118:109；104:109；123:109；105:92；105:106。第五場最後幾秒險輸。第六場最後幾秒險贏。

8.3　*Tunes of Purity and Peace*

The NBA Champion Toronto Raptors

June 13, 2019

Wolfpack of the Northern Raptors,

Firm and indomitable Canadian disruptors.

Round five is supposed to give the winning whistle,

Until the last moment of the one-point dismissal.

Suddenly all Canadians start to cry,

The dynasty of Warriors can no longer fly,

Chinese and Western are of the same thinking,

You are the King if you are the team of winning.

Scores of the first five games for the 2019 NBA Finals between Toronto Raptors and Golden State Warriors: 118:109; 104: 109; 123:109; 105:92; and 105:106. Golden State wins Game 5 in the final seconds. Toronto wins Game 6 in the final seconds.

虞　美　人
yú　　měi　　rén

德　克　薩　斯　式　的　放　縱
dé　kè　sà　sī　shì　de　fàng　zòng

2019　年　7　月　29　日

駕　車　閑　遊　休　斯　頓　，
jià　chē　xián　yóu　xiū　sī　dùn

易　把　高　路　混　。
yì　bǎ　gāo　lù　hùn

出　來　卻　還　在　裏　面　，
chū　lái　què　hái　zài　lǐ　miàn

上　去　猶　惑　不　知　在　外　邊　。
shàng　qù　yóu　huò　bú　zhī　zài　wài　biān

地　大　烤　辣　車　飛　快　，
dì　dà　kǎo　là　chē　fēi　kuài

牛　仔　多　豪　邁　。
niú　zǎi　duō　háo　mài

暢　飲　大　嚼　放　松　中　，
chàng　yǐn　dà　jiáo　fàng　sōng　zhōng

來　把　瀟　灑　德　州　式　放　縱　。
lái　bǎ　xiāo　sǎ　dé　zhōu　shì　fàng　zòng

8.4 *Poppy Beauty*

Indulgence of Texas Style

July 29, 2019

Driving on the Texas highway,

I would easily go astray.

Still on it thinking I am out,

Surely on it I start to grow doubt.

Land is vast,

Food is bold,

And cars are like tanks zooming about.

The cowboy things give you a knockout.

Pitch and pitch of chilled pale.

Burgers and wings are super-size in scale.

Love the indulgence of Texas style,

Drinking and eating always come with smile.

金　縷　曲
jīn　lǚ　qǔ

說　愁
shuō　chóu

2019　年　9　月　21　日

久　外　愛　懷　舊　。
jiǔ　wài　ài　huái　jiù

年　漸　長　、　不　分　冬　秋　，
nián　jiàn　zhǎng　　　bú　fēn　dōng　qiū

憂　體　不　瘦　。
yōu　tǐ　bú　shòu

見　故　想　往　易　心　動　，
jiàn　gù　xiǎng　wǎng　yì　xīn　dòng

涕　淚　浸　濕　衫　袖　。
tì　lèi　jìn　shī　shān　xiù

看　眼　前　、　國　度　紛　擾　，
kàn　yǎn　qián　　　guó　dù　fēn　rǎo

料　族　後　了　無　前　景　，
liào　zú　hòu　le　wú　qián　jǐng

油　然　生　、　滿　地　一　片　愁　。
yóu　rán　shēng　　　mǎn　dì　yī　piàn　chóu

細　思　恐　，　感　如　潮　。
xì　sī　kǒng　　　gǎn　rú　cháo

8.5.1 *Tune of Gold Thread*

Sentimental

September 21, 2019

Living afar goes with nostalgia,

Age grows regardless of Autumn or Winter.

It starts to be sentimental,

When your attention to shape becomes central.

Seeing the old friends and thinking the past,

It lets out tears very fast.

Worries and concerns are like overcast,

Some have passed and some will long last.

Looking at the chaotic present,

There is no good future for Asian descendant.

Thinking carefully about the prospect,

There is no good aspect that we would expect.

8.5.2　金縷曲
jīn　　lǚ　　qǔ

說愁
shuō　chóu

2019 年 9 月 21 日

常把酒來澆。
cháng bǎ jiǔ lái jiāo

異國遊、年來苦樂，
yì guó yóu　nián lái kǔ lè

隨波逐流。
suí bō zhú liú

多管自家門前雪，
duō guǎn zì jiā mén qián xuě

遇外內斂遷就。
yù wài nèi liǎn qiān jiù

數人頭、國人太少。
shù rén tóu　guó rén tài shǎo

偶聞族人試參政，
ǒu wén zú rén shì cān zhèng

欣喜余、遠遠不夠。
xīn xǐ yú　yuǎn yuǎn bú gòu

何時有、愁見頭？
hé shí yǒu　chóu jiàn tóu

8.5.2 *Tune of Gold Thread*

Sentimental

September 21, 2019

Wine may be fine in relieving concern.

There are bitterness and joy in living in foreign land.

Go with the flow and follow every turn,

Things that are different become easy to learn.

Asian culture focusing self-improvement inside,

Turn introverted to accommodate outside.

Good citizens cherish pride,

Need more people to participate and decide.

Too few Asian people try politics.

Great to hear people jump in with chopsticks.

The future is slim and it's way insufficient,

Not seeing the path when folks are proficient.

漁家傲
yú　jiā　ào

佛羅裏達
fó　luó　lǐ　dá

2019 年 9 月 26 日

長年高於七十度，
cháng nián gāo yú qī shí dù

不知冰雪為何物。
bú zhī bīng xuě wéi hé wù

海浪白灘棕櫚樹，
hǎi làng bái tān zōng lú shù

光腳蹼，
guāng jiǎo pǔ

多是渾圓便便腹。
duō shì hún yuán biàn biàn fù

人生棲息歡遊處，
rén shēng qī xī huān yóu chù

天上玉皇嘆不如。
tiān shàng yù huáng tàn bú rú

難怪川普買海湖，
nán guài chuān pǔ mǎi hǎi hú

颶風陸，
jù fēng lù

去了舒服來了苦。
qù le shū fú lái le kǔ

8.6 *Fisherman's Pride*

Florida

September 26, 2019

Warmer than 70 degrees all year long,

Snow and ice do not belong.

Waves and palm trees sing along,

Swim with fins in a beach throng.

Round bellies are big and strong,

The rich and powerful can't go wrong.

The place of joy and leisure,

When life no longer needs tenure.

Even the Jade Emperor envies the pleasure,

Mar-a-Lago is the golden measure.

Only if hurricanes disappear,

There would be no more sufferer.

8.7.1　　　江　城　子　　　　　　64
jiāng　　chéng　　zǐ

橄　欖　球　賽
gǎn　lǎn　qiú　sài

2019　年　11　月　11　日

眾　期　待　橄　欖　球　賽　，
zhòng　qī　dài　gǎn　lǎn　qiú　sài

九　人　隊　，　不　曾　敗　。
jiǔ　rén　duì　　bú　céng　bài

海　鷹　展　翅　，
hǎi　yīng　zhǎn　chì

愛　與　強　者　懟　。
ài　yǔ　qiáng　zhě　duì

輸　贏　勝　負　不　可　猜　，
shū　yíng　shèng　fù　bú　kě　cāi

時　候　對　，　運　自　來　。
shí　hòu　duì　　yùn　zì　lái

8.7.1　*Tune of Yangtze River City*

The Football Game

November 11, 2019

It's the most anticipated Seahawks' game.
The 49ers had the winning streak claim.
Hawk like Seattle hometown team,
Loved to play against the strong name.

Winning gets the fame,
Losing becomes lame.
Luck is often used to blame.
Great plays let no one in shame.

8.7.2　　　江　城　子
jiāng　　chéng　　zǐ

橄　欖　球　賽
gǎn　lǎn　qiú　sài

2019　年　11　月　11　日

海　鷹　欲　把　香　檳　開　，
hǎi　yīng　yù　bǎ　xiāng　bīn　kāi

臨　哨　吹　，　把　門　踹　。
lín　shào　chuī　　bǎ　mén　chuài

錯　愕　驚　呆　，
cuò　è　jīng　dāi

延　時　決　厲　害　。
yán　shí　jué　lì　hài

你　時　我　運　互　疊　代　，
nǐ　shí　wǒ　yùn　hù　dié　dài

雷　聲　喊　，　太　精　彩　。
léi　shēng　hǎn　　tài　jīng　cǎi

8.7.2　*Tune of Yangtze River City*

The Football Game

November 11, 2019

Victory came close for Seahawks to proclaim,

The 49ers never gave in being tame.

The last minute saw the relighted flame,

Achieving draw was the ultimate aim.

Overtime eventually came.

God's hand is always the same.

Losing could also proudly exclaim,

As long as it's a great game.

觀　橄　欖　球　賽
guān　gǎn　lǎn　qiú　sài

2019　年　11　月　11　日

察　看　年　度　球　賽　程　，
chá　kàn　nián　dù　qiú　sài　chéng

不　敗　僅　剩　金　九　人　。
bú　bài　jǐn　shèng　jīn　jiǔ　rén

首　戰　勁　敵　西　海　鷹　，
shǒu　zhàn　jìn　dí　xī　hǎi　yīng

驚　心　動　魄　似　要　贏　。
jīng　xīn　dòng　pò　sì　yào　yíng

西　圖　球　迷　本　要　慶　，
xī　tú　qiú　mí　běn　yào　qìng

哪　知　鳴　金　見　球　平　。
nǎ　zhī　míng　jīn　jiàn　qiú　píng

八贏不敗的舊金山四十九人（媒體愛稱九人隊），迎戰七贏二輸的西雅圖海鷹。眼看海鷹第四節 24：21 快要贏，哪知 49 人新手最後一分把球進。擲幣定奪加時進攻誰先行，幸運海鷹只要得分就算勝。誰料海鷹進攻被截停，再幸 49 人點球進攻沒有進。機會三次返回給海鷹，終長距進攻 27：24 一點球險勝。早就該贏，只可憐西雅圖球迷一顆懸心！

8.8.1　Watch the Football Game

November 11, 2019

Looking at the seasonal football roster,

Only team that has not had a loss was the 49er.

Meeting Seahawks was the season's first encounter,

The excitement was built up as high as ever.

It looked Seahawks was about to win,

The fans were ready for celebrating.

A last-minute twist suddenly came in.

The 49ers' field goal made the winning hope thin.

With eight wins and no loss, the San Francisco 49ers played against the seven-win and two-loss Seattle Seahawks. The Seahawks were on the way to win the game 24:21 at the last minute. Suddenly, the game was plunged into draw with the 49ers' field goal during the last seconds. In Overtime, whoever scores first wins the game. Seahawks was lucky enough to start offense first. Dramatically, it was intercepted by the 49ers. Even more bizarrely, the 49ers did not make the field goal, resulting in the third opportunity for Seahawks. The Seahawks ultimately won the game, only with the "12" fans' hearts always hanging in the air.

8.8.2

觀　橄　欖　球　賽
guān　gǎn　lǎn　qiú　sài

2019　年　11　月　11　日

加　時　得　分　就　算　勝　，
jiā　shí　dé　fèn　jiù　suàn　shèng

海　鷹　抽　籤　攻　先　行　。
hǎi　yīng　chōu　qiān　gōng　xiān　xíng

誰　料　臨　勝　又　截　停　，
shuí　liào　lín　shèng　yòu　jié　tíng

九　人　點　球　鴉　鵲　聲　。
jiǔ　rén　diǎn　qiú　yā　què　shēng

機　會　三　次　幸　光　臨　，
jī　huì　sān　cì　xìng　guāng　lín

堅　韌　不　拔　定　佳　音　。
jiān　rèn　bú　bá　dìng　jiā　yīn

8.8.2　Watch the Football Game

November 11, 2019

The regular time was a tie,

The overtime would make fans cry.

First scorer will make everyone say goodbye,

Seahawks were lucky to have the offense try.

Who thought of intercept?

49ers' field goal would let fans really upset.

Luck again gave the Seahawks fans' hope kept,

The third chance won back the Seahawks' respect.

白　種　人　黃　種　人
bái　zhǒng　rén　huáng　zhǒng　rén

2020　年　6　月　26　日

馬　可　波　羅　利　瑪　竇　，
mǎ　kě　bō　luó　lì　mǎ　dòu

跋　山　渡　水　中　國　遊　。
bá　shān　dù　shuǐ　zhōng　guó　yóu

庭　外　樹　齊　稻　花　香　，
tíng　wài　shù　qí　dào　huā　xiāng

湖　畔　村　綠　江　河　流　。
hú　pàn　cūn　lù　jiāng　hé　liú

溫　文　爾　雅　發　黑　亮　，
wēn　wén　ěr　yǎ　fā　hēi　liàng

錦　羅　緞　衣　白　臉　龐　，
jǐn　luó　duàn　yī　bái　liǎn　páng

自　嘆　發　粗　膚　蠟　黃　，
zì　tàn　fā　cū　fū　là　huáng

白　膚　色　人　在　東　方　。
bái　fū　sè　rén　zài　dōng　fāng

8.9.1　White People and Yellow People

June 26, 2020

Marco Polo and Matteo Ricci,

Travelled to ancient China from city to city.

Writing down what they were able to see,

They told the world an incredible story.

Outside of the beautiful residence court,

Full of flower scent of every sort.

Lakeside village surrounded by orderly trees,

Meandering river goes through town with breeze.

Gentle and civilized people have fine black hair,

With white skin face and wear silk attire.

Signed self of yellow skin like a beast,

White-skinned people are in the East.

8.9.2　　　　白　種　人　黃　種　人
　　　　　　　bái　zhǒng　rén　huáng　zhǒng　rén

2020　年　6　月　26　日

富　庶　華　麗　庭　院　深　，
fù　shù　huá　lì　tíng　yuàn　shēn

方　石　為　地　房　幾　淨　。
fāng　shí　wéi　dì　fáng　jǐ　jìng

白　如　奶　汁　滑　如　脂　，
bái　rú　nǎi　zhī　huá　rú　zhī

不　折　不　扣　白　色　人　。
bú　zhé　bú　kòu　bái　sè　rén

航　海　時　代　殖　民　盛　，
háng　hǎi　shí　dài　zhí　mín　shèng

工　業　革　命　清　人　治　，
gōng　yè　gé　mìng　qīng　rén　zhì

上　帝　嬌　子　白　種　人　，
shàng　dì　jiāo　zǐ　bái　zhǒng　rén

堅　船　利　炮　變　白　身　。
jiān　chuán　lì　pào　biàn　bái　shēn

8.9.2　White People and Yellow People

June 26, 2020

Land of the affluent and populous,

Home of the beautiful and gorgeous.

White as milk and smooth as silk,

These are the white people who are sleek.

Until the arrival of the voyage era,

The colonialism flourishes from afar.

Ruled by the Mandarin from Manchuria,

Ignoring the signal of industrialization flare.

God's prideful sons are the white,

The yellow switches side with a gunboat fight.

History is fact being wrong or right,

It's important to understand and gain insight.

8.9.3

白　種　人　黃　種　人
bái　zhǒng　rén　huáng　zhǒng　rén

2020　年　6　月　26　日

匈　奴　突　厥　蒙　滿　清　，
xiōng　nú　tū　jué　méng　mǎn　qīng

乍　然　崛　起　終　沈　寂　。
zhà　rán　jué　qǐ　zhōng　chén　jì

西　方　世　界　莫　跟　進　？
xī　fāng　shì　jiè　mò　gēn　jìn

唯　有　後　人　能　見　證　。
wéi　yǒu　hòu　rén　néng　jiàn　zhèng

民　族　文　化　多　如　星　，
mín　zú　wén　huà　duō　rú　xīng

歷　史　長　河　曇　花　現　。
lì　shǐ　cháng　hé　tán　huā　xiàn

傳　承　彌　新　方　歷　久　，
chuán　chéng　mí　xīn　fāng　lì　jiǔ

觀　天　之　道　執　天　行　。
guān　tiān　zhī　dào　zhí　tiān　xíng

8.9.3　White People and Yellow People

June 26, 2020

The Huns, Mongols and Manchurian,

Different tribes from the northern land.

Suddenly rise but shortly disband,

Melting into Middle Kingdom does not expand.

Would the Western world withstand?

We may not understand.

Things often happen not according to the planned,

Only future generations will see it firsthand.

Ethnic and cultures are full of variety.

Thousand years is short in the eye of history.

Sustaining needs both heritage and ingenuity.

Only following laws builds long lasting society.

夢 江 南
mèng　jiāng　nán

卡 羅 琳 娜 的 棒 球
kǎ　luó　lín　nà　de　bàng　qiú

2021 年 7 月 24 日

齊 韻 音 ，
qí　yùn　yīn

甜 蜜 卡 羅 琳 。
tián　mì　kǎ　luó　lín

再 融 似 水 南 國 情 ，
zài　róng　sì　shuǐ　nán　guó　qíng

今 昔 觸 動 多 少 心 。
jīn　xī　chù　dòng　duō　shǎo　xīn

不 禁 雙 淚 淋 。
bú　jìn　shuāng lèi　lín

8.10　*Dreaming the Yangtze River South*

South Carolina's Baseball Game

July 24, 2021

Harmonic tune alive,
Sweet Caroline,
The unencumbered heart line,
Makes the sun out and lets it shine.

With the Southern charm behind,
Like the dew on the vine,
Melting heart and mind,
With tears like rain.

水　調　歌　頭
shuǐ　diào　gē　tóu

南　國　北　國
nán　guó　běi　guó

2021　年　8　月　26　日

晴　空　萬　萬　裏　，
qíng　kōng　wàn　wàn　lǐ

火　辣　辣　太　陽　。
huǒ　là　là　tài　yáng

正　是　南　國　初　秋　，
zhèng　shì　nán　guó　chū　qiū

如　東　國　故　鄉　。
rú　dōng　guó　gù　xiāng

聳　立　寬　廣　路　橋　，
sǒng　lì　kuān　guǎng　lù　qiáo

超　量　份　大　牛　排　，
chāo　liàng　fèn　dà　niú　pái

處　處　是　豪　爽　。
chù　chù　shì　háo　shuǎng

科　技　新　貴　土　，
kē　jì　xīn　guì　tǔ

西　部　猶　粗　曠　。
xī　bù　yóu　cū　kuàng

8.11.1　*Prelude to the Water Melody*

Southern Land and Northern Land

August 26, 2021

The sky is crystal clear.

The sun is as hot as fire.

It's early Autumn in the southern land,

In the heart chunk of America.

Reminding me of the Yangtze River,

And the southern hometown in China.

The silk and flower,

The elegant and beautiful sun after shower.

Highrise bridges and broad roads,

Extra-large meals are in loads.

As Silicon Valley technology finds new abodes,

Everywhere you go is forthright and bold.

8.11.2

水　調　歌　頭
shuǐ　diào　gē　tóu

南　國　北　國
xià　rì　bīng　dǎo

2021　年　8　月　26　日

每　造　訪　，　喜　心　情　，
měi　zào　fǎng　　xǐ　xīn　qíng

總　難　忘　。
zǒng　nán　wàng

不　眠　西　村　柔　情　，
bú　mián　xī　cūn　róu　qíng

北　國　訴　衷　腸　。
běi　guó　sù　zhōng　cháng

南　國　北　國　迥　異　，
nán　guó　běi　guó　jiǒng　yì

西　方　東　方　雷　同　，
xī　fāng　dōng　fāng　léi　tóng

差　別　僅　鏡　像　。
chà　bié　jǐn　jìng　xiàng

水　土　各　一　方　，
shuǐ　tǔ　gè　yī　fāng

人　間　卻　一　樣　。
rén　jiān　què　yī　yàng

8.11.2　*Prelude to the Water Melody*

Southern Land and Northern Land

August 26, 2021

Every visit is incredible,
Happy mood is inevitable.
The experience is unbelievable.
It's always unforgettable.

Sleepless Seattle's tenderness,
It's the northern land's romantics.
North and South are so different,
East to West is much congruent.

Only difference is the mirror opposite,
Country to country and site to site.
Water and soil with the territory claim,
The world is essentially all the same.

臨　江　仙
lín　jiāng　xiān

五　套　餐
wǔ　tào　cān

2021　年　12　月　2　日

生　活　方　式　首　論　舌　，
shēng　huó　fāng　shì　shǒu　lùn　shé

美　酒　美　食　常　談　。
měi　jiǔ　měi　shí　cháng　tán

流　行　最　數　五　套　餐　。
liú　xíng　zuì　shù　wǔ　tào　cān

三　臺　把　胃　開　，
sān　tái　bǎ　wèi　kāi

主　盤　再　甜　點　。
zhǔ　pán　zài　tián　diǎn

面　包　橄　欖　波　爾　多　，
miàn　bāo　gǎn　lǎn　bō　ěr　duō

蟹　糕　色　拉　蔬　鮮　。
xiè　gāo　sè　lā　shū　xiān

沖　浪　草　原　布　蕾　添　，
chōng　làng　cǎo　yuán　bù　lěi　tiān

起　終　皆　法　國　，
qǐ　zhōng　jiē　fǎ　guó

與　中　華　比　肩　。
yǔ　zhōng　huá　bǐ　jiān

8.12　*River Side Fairy*

Five Course Meal

December 2, 2021

Eating should come first in life quality.

Good food and wine are number one priority.

The most popular is the five-course meal.

It always has its greatest appeal.

With bread, olive oil and Bordeaux wine,

The dessert of the heart-melting kind.

Three courses of appetizer kick off hunger desire.

The main course would make you want to retire.

Fresh vegetable salad and crab cake,

Surf and turf with the Brulé bake.

Starting with French and ending with French,

Rivals with the Chinese Emperor's royal dish.

9 國 外 生 活
guó　wài　shēng　huó

LIVING ABROAD

9.1.1　　如 夢 令
　　　　　rú　mèng　lìng

說 忙
shuō　máng

2019 年 9 月 7 日

電　郵　堆　積　如　山　，
diàn　yóu　duī　jī　rú　shān

吃　飯　仍　須　買　單　。
chī　fàn　réng　xū　mǎi　dān

孩　童　四　處　躥　，
hái　tóng　sì　chù　cuān

弄　壞　自　己　衣　衫　。
nòng　huài　zì　jǐ　yī　shān

快　點　，　快　點　，
kuài　diǎn　　kuài　diǎn

總　是　沒　有　時　間　。
zǒng　shì　méi　yǒu　shí　jiān

9.1.1　*Short Tune of Dreaming*

Being Busy

September 7, 2019

Emails can get you drowned,
Still need to pay for the hash brown.
Rules and conditions let you bound,
Good ways are not easy to be found.

Children love to jump up and down,
Messing all things on the ground.
"Hurry, hurry" comes the screaming sound.
There is no time to fool around.

9.1.2　　　如　　夢　　令
　　　　　　　rú　　mèng　　lìng

　　　說　　忙
　　　shuō　　máng

2019　年　9　月　7　日

庭　院　廣　野　地　荒　，
tíng yuàn guǎng yě dì huāng

兩　鬢　更　見　侵　霜　。
liǎng bìn gèng jiàn qīn shuāng

西　村　又　夕　陽　，
xī cūn yòu xī yáng

路　艱　道　阻　且　長　。
lù jiān dào zǔ qiě cháng

太　忙　，　太　忙　，
tài máng tài máng

旅　途　老　出　狀　況　。
lǚ tú lǎo chū zhuàng kuàng

9.1.2 *Short Tune of Dreaming*

Being Busy

September 7, 2019

The courtyard and wide fields are untended,
The ever-grey sideburns can't be transcended.
With the fast and short day almost ended,
Wish there is time to get things mended.

The road is hard and extended,
Taking iterations to correct the unintended.
"Too busy, too busy" is not pretended,
Hoping the journey would be splendid.

夢　懷　千　秋
mèng　huái　qiān　qiū

2019　年　10　月　26　日

萬　裏　海　外　遊　，
wàn　lǐ　hǎi　wài　yóu

夢　懷　一　千　秋　。
mèng　huái　yī　qiān　qiū

客　居　三　十　載　，
kè　jū　sān　shí　zǎi

何　如　解　鄉　愁　？
hé　rú　jiě　xiāng　chóu

9.2 Dreaming a Thousand Autumns

October 26, 2019

Travel thousands of miles overseas,

Dreaming a thousand Autumns.

Living abroad for over thirty years,

How do you solve the homesickness?

水　調　歌　頭
shuǐ　diào　gē　tóu

三　個　生　日
sān　gè　shēng　rì

2019　年　11　月　4　日

陰　歷　十　月　三　，
yīn　lì　shí　yuè　sān

上　天　偏　降　我　。
shàng　tiān　piān　jiàng　wǒ

陽　歷　來　月　十　四　，
yáng　lì　lái　yuè　shí　sì

本　亦　無　不　妥　。
běn　yì　wú　bú　tuǒ

人　有　大　意　漏　疏　，
rén　yǒu　dà　yì　lòu　shū

字　有　魯　魚　亥　豕　，
zì　yǒu　lǔ　yú　hài　shǐ

戶　籍　出　差　錯　。
hù　jí　chū　chà　cuò

清　晰　生　辰　數　，
qīng　xī　shēng　chén　shù

竟　將　一　字　抹　。
jìng　jiāng　yī　zì　mò

9.3.1　*Prelude of the Water Melody*

Three Birthdays in the Same Year

November 4, 2019

October 3rd of the lunar calendar,

Sees me coming to this world as a traveler.

It's the fourteenth day of November.

Everything is good and proper.

Negligence is human nature,

Error is a common feature.

Mistake can be normal behavior.

Human being is not a strange creature.

It all pertains to the birth certificate registrar,

There is only one small error.

The birth date is abundantly clear,

Only with a thin number stripped forever.

9.3.2

水 調 歌 頭
shuǐ　diào　gē　tóu

三 個 生 日
sān　gè　shēng　rì

2019 年 11 月 4 日

差 一 字 ， 慶 三 次 ，
chà　yi　zì　　qìng　sān　cì

得 其 所 。
dé　qí　suǒ

蹉 跎 歲 月 ，
cuō　tuó　suì　yuè

逢 事 愛 把 酒 來 酌 。
féng　shì　ài　bǎ　jiǔ　lái　zhuó

人 生 固 有 差 池 ，
rén　shēng　gù　yǒu　chà　chí

不 可 預 知 禍 福 ，
bú　kě　yù　zhī　huò　fú

樂 把 生 日 過 。
lè　bǎ　shēng　rì　guò

無 須 理 繁 雜 ，
wú　xū　lǐ　fán　zá

飲 了 酒 再 說 。
yǐn　le　jiǔ　zài　shuō

9.3.2 *Prelude of the Water Melody*

Three Birthdays in the Same Year

November 4, 2019

The difference is only on one number,
The outcome is three times celebrating over.
That is exactly what one would like to occur,
You would very much wonder.

Time flies with month and year,
Drinking is into play when the occasion is near.
Life is inherently full of blunder,
It's hard to predict if it's worse or better.

Three birthdays always make one happier,
Put aside and ignore the distractor.
Raise for a toast and start another good cheer,
Let other things be dealt after.

破　陣　子
pò　zhèn　zǐ

三 十 寒 暑 海 外
sān shí hán shǔ hǎi wài

2020 年 8 月 28 日

三 十 寒 暑 海 外 ，
sān shí hán shǔ hǎi wài

八 千 裏 路 雲 海 。
bā qiān lǐ lù yún hǎi

域 外 世 界 多 精 彩 ，
yù wài shì jiè duō jīng cǎi

卻 不 敵 關 內 自 在 ，
què bú dí guān nèi zì zài

幾 度 長 城 塞 。
jǐ dù cháng chéng sāi

中 原 方 興 未 艾 ，
zhōng yuán fāng xìng wèi ài

西 方 日 薄 西 曬 。
xī fāng rì báo xī shài

好 漢 不 提 當 年 快 ，
hǎo hàn bú tí dāng nián kuài

洋 為 中 用 依 青 睞 ，
yáng wéi zhōng yòng yī qīng lài

何 不 故 裏 邁 ？
hé bú gù lǐ mài

9.4　*Tune of Breaking Battle Formation*

Thirty Years Overseas

August 28, 2020

Thirty years overseas living afar,

With eight-thousand-mile clouds and stars.

How wonderful the outside worlds are,

Not as at ease as hometown that I can swear.

How many times would you consider?

The unfolding and sweeping change era.

If history can serve as a reflecting mirror,

Riding the right wave can make you a winner.

Trend and tide are about big idea,

Western world declining is clear.

Mixing foreign with self makes great things appear,

Why not bring it all together?

懷　　舊
huái　　jiù

2020　年　10　月　2　日

西　村　山　彩　水　秀　，
xī　cūn　shān　cǎi　shuǐ　xiù

該　是　北　京　金　秋　。
gāi　shì　běi　jīng　jīn　qiū

兒　女　空　巢　時　候　，
ér　nǚ　kōng　cháo　shí　hòu

最　是　容　易　懷　舊　。
zuì　shì　róng　yì　huái　jiù

喜逢週末，情不自禁，填詞釋懷，念舊一把。

9.5　Thinking of the Past

October 2, 2020

Colorful trees and mountains,

Beautiful waters and fountains.

Seattle's early Autumn,

It's the best time before the raining.

It must be the golden time in Beijing,

With the red leaves all over the Fragrance Mountain.

The hardest is the beginning of the empty nest living,

That always brings back the past in the thinking.

It's lovely weekend time. Overwhelmed by the emotions, I started to write poems to release the feelings. It's a quick time of nostalgia.

江　城　子
jiāng　　chéng　　zǐ

憶　張　強
yì　zhāng　qiáng

2020　年　10　月　10　日

夜　來　幽　夢　返　真　光　，
yè　lái　yōu　mèng　fǎn　zhēn　guāng

多　少　趟　，　歡　聚　堂　。
duō　shǎo　tàng　　huān　jù　táng

同　齡　遊　子　，　西　圖　當　吾　鄉　。
tóng　líng　yóu　zǐ　　xī　tú　dāng　wú　xiāng

作　新　斯　人　動　四　方　，
zuò　xīn　sī　rén　dòng　sì　fāng

領　賢　榜　，　齊　家　樣　。
lǐng　xián　bǎng　　qí　jiā　yàng

忽　而　一　雷　驚　天　響　，
hū　ér　yī　léi　jīng　tiān　xiǎng

不　同　窗　，　常　同　享　。
bú　tóng　chuāng　　cháng　tóng　xiǎng

英　年　早　逝　，　心　中　淚　千　行　。
yīng　nián　zǎo　shì　　xīn　zhōng　lèi　qiān　háng

秋　風　細　雨　少　夕　陽　，
qiū　fēng　xì　yǔ　shǎo　xī　yáng

長　思　量　，　憶　張　強　。
cháng　sī　liàng　　yì　zhāng　qiáng

9.6　*Tune of Yangtze River City*

Remembering John Zhang

October 10, 2020

Dreaming to return to the church of True Light,
Where we all come and unite.
The numerous gatherings day and night.
Always continual sources of delight.

We are the same wave of travelers wandering around,
Settling in Seattle as our second hometown.
Your fresh presence is so profound,
Role models starting from you then we count down.

Suddenly a thunder shook the sky,
You left us all without saying goodbye.
Dying young with vitality high,
You let our hearts shed tears and cry.

Never being a colleague or of the same class,
We all do share the similar paths.
Drizzle with no sun is like fall's Seattle song.
We will sing it long and remember you strong.

上　帝　驕　子
shàng　dì　jiāo　zǐ

2020 年 12 月 12 日

馬　可　波　羅　，　奇　遊　中　國　。
mǎ　kě　bō　luó　　qí　yóu　zhōng guó

利　瑪　竇　，　言　亦　闊　綽　。
lì　mǎ　dòu　　yán　yì　kuò　chuò

樹　齊　花　香　，　河　繞　村　過　。
shù　qí　huā　xiāng　　hé　rào　cūn　guò

溫　文　爾　雅　，　頭　髮　黑　，
wēn　wén　ěr　yǎ　　tóu　fā　hēi

臉　似　帛　。
liǎn　sì　bó

自　嘆　毛　碩　，　膚　如　蠟　珀　。
zì　tàn　máo　shuò　　fū　rú　là　pò

白　色　人　，　世　界　東　末　。
bái　sè　rén　　shì　jiè　dōng　mò

歲　月　蹉　跎　，　鸞　飄　鳳　泊　。
suì　yuè　cuō　tuó　　luán　piāo　fèng　bó

上　帝　驕　子　，　白　種　人　，
shàng　dì　jiāo　zǐ　　bái　zhǒng　rén

本　你　我　。
běn　nǐ　wǒ

9.7 *Rite of Burning Incense*

God's Prideful Son

December 12, 2020

Marco Polo, the explorer,
Traveled to China to its corner.
Matteo Ricci, the preacher,
Hailed acclamation to great China.

Trees are aligned in great order,
Wafting the scent of flower.
Passing the village is a beautiful river,
People have white skin and black hair.

With hair thick and skin in tan,
The Westerns could not help lament.
The people of color of white,
Resided on the world's East side.

Years and months flew,
World tide started anew.
God's prideful son the white grew,
Supposed to be me and you.

采 桑 子
cǎi sāng zǐ

唐 人 華 人 中 國 人
táng rén huá rén zhōng guó rén

2020 年 12 月 31 日

唐 人 華 人 中 國 人 。
táng rén huá rén zhōng guó rén

天 涯 海 邊 ， 皆 謂 秦 人 。
tiān yá hǎi biān jiē wèi qín rén

西 人 不 分 東 方 顏 。
xī rén bú fèn dōng fāng yán

秦 人 本 就 虎 狼 般 。
qín rén běn jiù hǔ láng bān

道 儒 法 循 ， 神 通 各 顯 。
dào rú fǎ xún shén tōng gè xiǎn

不 分 莫 把 秦 人 怨 。
bú fèn mò bǎ qín rén yuàn

Chinese 是唐人，華人，中國人。而在異域，從古至今，只有秦人。

9.8 *Mulberry Picking*

The Chinese

December 31, 2020

From the streets of the Tang people,

To the corners of the world,

Living afar or close to homeland,

Chinese are alike even as nomad.

Wherever their origin,

By the Western thinking paradigm,

All are from the same region,

As the people of ancient Qin.

Outside does not discern the Eastern,

Ancient Qin people are quite stern.

With Taoist, Confucianist, and Legalist born,

Not telling difference can be a huge concern.

憶 江 南
yì jiāng nán

綠 頌
lù sòng

2021 年 2 月 8 日

西 村 綠 ，
xī cūn lù

勿 須 春 風 度 。
wù xū chūn fēng dù

長 年 蘭 花 秋 天 菊 ，
cháng nián lán huā qiū tiān jú

不 比 江 南 青 梅 竹 。
bú bǐ jiāng nán qīng méi zhú

常 念 綠 茶 樹 。
cháng niàn lù chá shù

生日快樂!

9.9 *Reminiscing the Yangtze River South*

Ode to Green

February 8, 2021

The evergreens of Seattle,

Never wait for Spring's arrival.

Like a city for emerald,

Seattle does not have a rival.

Chrysanthemum's Autumn blossom,

Orchid all year bloom,

Never have a matching room,

To the bamboo and green plum.

Take a river south roam,

It's better than touring Rome.

The green tea tree is mesmerizing,

From the south China home.

Happy Birthday!

又　逢　生　季
yòu　féng　shēng　jì

2021　年　11　月　4　日

羈　旅　遠　歸　，
jī　lǚ　yuǎn　guī

不　蓋　由　己　，
bú　gài　yóu　jǐ

勞　歇　依　按　東　時　。
láo　xiē　yī　àn　dōng　shí

倚　枕　而　憩　鬧　鐘　驚　，
yǐ　zhěn　ér　qì　nào　zhōng　jīng

上　虛　擬　、　奔　夜　趕　日　。
shàng　xū　nǐ　bēn　yè　gǎn　rì

不　用　回　首　，
bú　yòng　huí　shǒu

只　須　照　鏡　，
zhī　xū　zhào　jìng

兩　鬢　滄　桑　盡　溢　。
liǎng　bìn　cāng　sāng　jìn　yì

人　生　路　長　有　豐　盈　，
rén　shēng　lù　cháng　yǒu　fēng　yíng

陋　屋　變　、　摘　星　華　室　。
lòu　wū　biàn　zhāi　xīng　huá　shì

9.10 *Fairy on the Magpie Bridge*

The Season of Birthdays

November 4, 2021

Return home from a far-away trip,
Many things are out of your grip.
Work and rest in the time of East,
Bio clock is not easy to flip.

Alarm sound more like a whip,
Natural awakening is rare with sleep.
Back to bustling of the virtual world,
Birthday greetings just a life blip.

Experience is never a skip,
Perseverance grows from hardship.
No need to look back with reflection,
Life is a rich journey from the crib.

Chances come and slip,
Ups often go with dip.
It's another beautiful birthday,
When stars pop out a pinata rip.

玉　樓　春
yù　lóu　chūn

夢　遊　東　瀛
mèng　yóu　dōng　yíng

2021　年　12　月　31　日

長　聞　日　人　論　華　夏　，
cháng　wén　rì　rén　lùn　huá　xià

崖　山　之　後　無　中　華　。
yá　shān　zhī　hòu　wú　zhōng　huá

踏　著　鐵　鞋　島　上　尋　，
tà　zhe　tiě　xié　dǎo　shàng　xún

唐　時　廟　宇　宋　時　塔　。
táng　shí　miào　yǔ　sòng　shí　tǎ

蒙　滿　本　就　一　檐　下　，
méng　mǎn　běn　jiù　yī　yán　xià

只　是　還　把　和　韓　差　。
zhī　shì　hái　bǎ　hé　hán　chà

寰　宇　滿　是　東　方　顏　，
huán　yǔ　mǎn　shì　dōng　fāng　yán

真　正　中　華　在　老　家　。
zhēn　zhèng　zhōng　huá　zài　lǎo　jiā

9.11　*Spring of the Jade Tower*

Japan Visit in a Dream

December 31, 2021

Often heard Japanese talking about ancient China,
Real China was gone after the War of Mount Ya.
Looking for traces of old China everywhere,
There are Chinese things like temple and pagoda.

Manchuria and Mongolia are under one umbrella,
Only missing members are Japan and Korea.
Chinese visitors filling the world more than ever,
True China only exists in its home backyard.

10 第二故鄉

dì　èr　gù　xiāng

SECOND HOMETOWN

酹　江　月
lèi　jiāng　yuè

三　雪
sān　xuě

2019　年　2　月　9　日

北　國　風　光　，
běi　guó　fēng　guāng

雪　皚　皚　、爭　比　綠　樹　鋒　芒　。
xuě　ái　ái　　zhēng　bǐ　lù　shù　fēng　máng

坡　多　路　滑　城　癱　瘓　，
pō　duō　lù　huá　chéng　tān　huàn

衙　府　瞪　眼　恐　慌　。
yá　fǔ　dèng　yǎn　kǒng　huāng

冰　雪　世　界　，
bīng　xuě　shì　jiè

本　是　妖　嬈　，
běn　shì　yāo　ráo

只　把　急　旨　降　。
zhǐ　bǎ　jí　zhǐ　jiàng

閉　門　鎖　戶　，
bì　mén　suǒ　hù

坐　等　天　暖　來　幫　。
zuò　děng　tiān　nuǎn　lái　bāng

10.1.1 *Libation to the Moon River*

Three Snows

February 9, 2019

A common scene of the northern land,

The white snow is rarely so grand.

Standing out from the white beach sand,

Compete with the trees of emerald city brand.

With roads slippery and city shut down,

Government couldn't help but only frown.

Snow and ice would make a wonder town,

Officials only had emergency to announce.

Close the door and shut the gate,

Nothing else to do but patently wait.

It's the weather that decided the fate,

Hoping the warm air did not come too late.

10.1.2

醉 江 月
lèi jiāng yuè

三 雪
sān xuě

2019 年 2 月 9 日

波 城 漫 天 凝 雨 ，
bō chéng màn tiān níng yǔ

不 慌 不 忙 ，
bú huāng bú máng

無 論 雪 與 霜 。
wú lùn xuě yǔ shuāng

西 村 或 無 治 寒 策 ，
xī cūn huò wú zhì hán cè

翠 城 確 少 此 況 。
cuì chéng què shǎo cǐ kuàng

隔 日 再 雪 ， 童 雀 二 喜 ，
gé rì zài xuě tóng què èr xǐ

又 無 學 堂 上 。
yòu wú xué táng shàng

晴 日 預 報 ，
qíng rì yù bào

三 喜 一 周 在 望 。
sān xǐ yī zhōu zài wàng

波城：波士頓

10.1.2 *Libation to the Moon River*

Three Snows

February 9, 2019

In the Boston days where this happened,
People were not frightened or concerned.
Being freezing rain or heavy snow,
There were always ways to easily handle.

Not because Seattle lacks skill,
Things like this do not frequently show.
Next day forecasted with another snow,
Kids happily yell with more no school bell.

Another day goes by with sunny sky,
New forecast will make officials cry.
In about a week's time,
There will be the 3rd snow surprise.

夏　日
xià　　　rì

2019 年 7 月 20 日

極 目 山 峰 眺 四 方 ，
jí mù shān fēng tiào sì fāng

疑 是 明 媚 春 日 光 。
yí shì míng mèi chūn rì guāng

晨 霧 輕 漫 平 湖 上 ，
chén wù qīng màn píng hú shàng

錯 把 西 圖 當 蘇 杭 。
cuò bǎ xī tú dāng sū háng

10.2　Summer Day

July 20, 2019

Eyes looking afar from mountain pinnacle,

Spring sunshine in Summer is mythical.

Morning mist flowing over lake with no obstacle,

Mistaking Seattle for Hangzhou and Suzhou.

空 中 機 上
kōng zhōng jī shàng

2019 年 9 月 19 日

空 中 機 上 ， 閑 坐 正 凝 想 。
kōng zhōng jī shàng   xián zuò zhèng níng xiǎng

知 天 命 ， 耳 順 暢 。
zhī tiān mìng   ěr shùn chàng

世 事 幾 多 愁 ， 江 水 東 流 長 。
shì shì jǐ duō chóu   jiāng shuǐ dōng liú cháng

把 酒 點 ， 亞 當 姆 斯 腹 中 晃 。
bǎ jiǔ diǎn   yà dāng mǔ sī fù zhōng huǎng

瑣 碎 放 一 旁 ， 夢 裏 寫 文 章 。
suǒ suì fàng yī páng   mèng lǐ xiě wén zhāng

思 緒 廣 ， 勿 迷 茫 。
sī xù guǎng   wù mí máng

低 頭 看 外 窗 ， 一 片 好 風 光 。
dī tóu kàn wài chuāng   yī piàn hǎo fēng guāng

高 處 望 ， 運 籌 帷 幄 定 安 邦 。
gāo chù wàng   yùn chóu wéi wò dìng ān bāng

亞當姆斯：Samuel Adams，波士頓產啤酒。

10.3　*Year of Thousand Autumns*

Flying Back Home

September 19, 2019

On the plane and in the air,

Thinking deep and sitting idle in the chair.

Knowing your destiny,

Makes you much be aware.

Ask how many worries you bear,

It's like a long East flowing river.

Only after you order a beer,

You start to be bold and dare.

Laying aside the trivia,

Dream of writing articles at leisure.

Thinking out of square,

Let yourself be completely bare.

Looking down the airplane exterior,

There is a beautiful scenery of world fanfare.

Only looking from a place higher,

You can see things in a big picture.

2020 年 5 月 12 日

杳杳故土，
江南秀竹。
浩氣天祥，
擎天如柱。

纖纖西圖，
不分雲霧。
山高海闊，
豁達大度。

10.4　Sleek Seattle

May 12, 2020

Far away the old hometown land,

Beautiful bamboo forest to the south riverbank.

The vast noble spirit of the hometown hero,

Higher into the sky than the pyramid of pharaoh.

Slim and sleek new hometown Seattle,

Telling fog from cloud needs a battle.

With mountain high and ocean wide,

Comes with the broad mind and generous pride.

凌　波　曲
líng　bō　qǔ

初　夏
chū　xià

2020 年 5 月 12 日

千　紅　萬　綠　，
qiān　hóng　wàn　lǜ

春　色　猶　駐　，
chūn　sè　yóu　zhù

氣　爽　日　麗　光　媚　，
qì　shuǎng　rì　lì　guāng　mèi

漫　天　花　飛　絮　。
màn　tiān　huā　fēi　xù

羅　裳　衣　輕　，
luó　shang　yī　qīng

飄　然　幽　徑　，
piāo　rán　yōu　jìng

堪　比　昆　侖　瑤　池　，
kān　bǐ　kūn　lún　yáo　chí

人　間　夢　仙　境　。
rén　jiān　mèng　xiān　jìng

10.5　*Tune of Ripple Dancing*

Seattle's Early Summer

May 12, 2020

One thousand reds and ten thousand greens,
The color of Spring is still the scene.
Cool refreshing air and warm sunshine,
Relaxing catkins floating high in sky.

With skirt bright and clothing light,
Walking the secluded path like a fairy sprite.
Like the Jade Lake on the Kunlun Mountain,
The paradise of the world ever in dreaming.

南　煙
nán　　yān

2020 年 10 月 1 日

西　村　中　秋　天　堂　臨　，
xī　cūn　zhōng　qiū　tiān　táng　lín

遠　目　遙　南　又　煙　塵　。
yuǎn　mù　yáo　nán　yòu　yān　chén

問　君　誰　把　月　兒　欺　，
wèn　jūn　shuí　bǎ　yuè　ér　qī

紅　臉　羞　見　加　州　人　。
hóng　liǎn　xiū　jiàn　jiā　zhōu　rén

10.6　Southern Smoke

October 1, 2020

Paradise arrived in Seattle to celebrate Mid-Autumn,

Until smoke came from America's south bottom.

Ask the moon who bullied her the awesome,

Timidly pointing to the California as the problem.

洞　仙　歌
dòng　xiān　gē

秋　雨
qiū　yǔ

2019 年 10 月 17 日

西　風　送　夏　，
xī　fēng　sòng　xià

雲　霧　繞　萬　家　。
yún　wù　rào　wàn　jiā

綿　綿　秋　雨　淅　淅　下　。
mián　mián　qiū　yǔ　xī　xī　xià

登　望　遠　，
dēng　wàng　yuǎn

常　綠　松　杉　遍　野　，
cháng　lù　sōng　shān　biàn　yě

天　河　轉　，
tiān　hé　zhuǎn

春　秋　日　照　無　差　。
chūn　qiū　rì　zhào　wú　chà

10.7.1 *Song of the Cave Fairy*

Autumn Rain

October 17, 2019

The west wind sends off Summer,

With clouds filling the air,

And fogs over hill and dale,

The Autumn drizzles start to whisper.

Stand high and look far,

Evergreen pine and fir are everywhere.

The ever-rotating planet and star,

Spring and Autumn sun rays are never apart.

10.7.2
洞　仙　歌
dòng　xiān　gē

秋　雨
qiū　yǔ

2019　年　10　月　17　日

觀　庭　中　黃　花　，
guān　tíng　zhōng　huáng　huā

煙　雨　朦　朧　，
yān　yǔ　méng　lóng

更　像　梅　雨　江　南　灑　。
gèng　xiàng　méi　yǔ　jiāng　nán　sǎ

功　名　趁　年　華　，
gōng　míng　chèn　nián　huá

低　首　勤　作　，
dī　shǒu　qín　zuò

翠　城　人　，　雨　季　最　佳　。
cuì　chéng　rén　　yǔ　jì　zuì　jiā

秋　如　故　人　雨　似　故　國　，
qiū　rú　gù　rén　yǔ　sì　gù　guó

又　輪　新　水　再　試　新　茶　。
yòu　lún　xīn　shuǐ　zài　shì　xīn　chá

10.7.2　*Song of the Cave Fairy*

Autumn Rain

October 17, 2019

Look at the garden's yellow flower,

And the misty rain shower.

It's more like the Plum Rain,

Sprinkling in the south of the Yangtze River.

Great achievement goes with starting young.

With the heads down,

People work all raining season long,

The Emerald City success is hard-won.

Autumn is like an old friend we often see,

Rain is like that from the old country

Another round of new water,

It's a new kind of tea.

暴　風
bào　　fēng

2021 年 1 月 13 日

一　夜　疾　風　度　，
yī　yè　jí　fēng　dù

斷　電　千　萬　戶　，
duàn　diàn　qiān　wàn　hù

時　光　穿　如　梭　，
shí　guāng　chuān　rú　suō

燭　光　照　千　古　。
zhú　guāng　zhào　qiān　gǔ

昨日晚上，西雅圖一年一兩次的暴風雨，致五十萬戶斷電失網。宛如一夜回到百年前。甚是感慨。

10.8　Storm Wind

January 13, 2021

One warm winter night,

Blowing the gusty wind fright.

Tens of thousands of homes,

Losing power and sight.

Time flies by,

At the blink of an eye.

Shining through the ages,

The thousand-year candlelight.

Last night a storm of once or twice a year ripped through Western Washington, leaving half million homes without power. It's like we were suddenly brought back to the ages of candlelight. The feeling was so compelling that I started to write down my experience.

春　雪
chūn　xuě

2021 年 2 月 13 日

新　年　猶　未　有　芳　華　，
xīn　nián　yóu　wèi　yǒu　fāng　huá

正　月　乍　驚　看　嫩　芽　，
zhèng　yuè　zhà　jīng　kàn　nèn　yá

白　雪　都　嫌　春　來　晚　，
bái　xuě　dōu　xián　chūn　lái　wǎn

飛　穿　庭　樹　做　絮　花　。
fēi　chuān　tíng　shù　zuò　xù　huā

西雅圖今冬的第一場大雪，從大年初一開始，下到初二、初三。望雪生情，改韓愈《春雪》。

10.9　Spring Snow

February 13, 2021

The late Chinese New Year,

Still has no fragrance of Spring flower.

It's surprising in the first moon,

To see the buds before the bloom.

The snow can no longer wait,

With Spring being late.

Flying through the tree with spirals,

Pretending to be flower petals.

雪　　夜
xuě　　yè

2021 年　2　月　13　日

月　照　雪　夜　清　，
yuè zhào xuě yè qīng

燈　熄　窗　更　明　，
dēng xī chuāng gèng míng

定　是　送　春　來　，
dìng shì sòng chūn lái

天　亮　猶　不　停　。
tiān liàng yóu bú tíng

10.10　Snow Night

February 13, 2021

The moon shines on the snow,

In a night that is clear and cold.

With windows open and lights out,

It's so bright to see all whereabout.

The way to say welcome,

For Spring to finally come.

White snow the awesome,

Not stopping even when it's dawn.

瑞 雪
ruì xuě

2021 年 2 月 13 日

豐 年 好 大 雪，
fēng nián hǎo dà xuě

萬 蟲 跡 皆 絕，
wàn chóng jì jiē jué

邁 步 入 牛 年，
mài bù rù niú nián

好 兆 新 年 躍。
hǎo zhào xīn nián yuè

10.11　Auspicious Snow

February 13, 2021

Heavy snow for an abundance year,

With all insects that will disappear.

Stepping into the year of the ox,

Good omen for good year of crops.

霜　天　冬　曉
shuāng　tiān　dōng　xiǎo

2021　年　11　月　17　日

雲　海　茫　茫　遮　波　濤　，
yún　hǎi　máng　máng　zhē　bō　tāo

青　山　耀　耀　東　方　曉　，
qīng　shān　yào　yào　dōng　fāng　xiǎo

滿　目　秋　林　屋　上　霜　，
mǎn　mù　qiū　lín　wū　shàng　shuāng

原　是　西　村　晴　冬　早　。
yuán　shì　xī　cūn　qíng　dōng　zǎo

10.12　Winter Dawn of a Frosty Day

November 17, 2021

In a dawn of clear manifest,

With sunshine out of mountain crest,

The sea of meandering clouds,

It's winter morning in Seattle's best.

White frost coming as rooftop guest,

Still in green Autumn Forest,

Misty fog and down under lake,

All are wonders full of zest.

11　哲　學

zhé　　xué

PHILOSOPHY

上　帝　永　恒　非　萬　能
shàng　dì　yǒng　héng　fēi　wàn　néng

2020　年　5　月　9　日

始　止　觀　。
shǐ　zhǐ　guān

絕　對　寰　宇　不　存　。
jué　duì　huán　yǔ　bú　cún

絕　不　存　，　其　成　悖　論　，
jué　bú　cún　　qí　chéng　bèi　lùn

絕　對　存　在　可　定　斷　。
jué　duì　cún　zài　kě　dìng　duàn

萬　物　皆　變　換　。
wàn　wù　jiē　biàn　huàn

變　更　。　唯　一　不　變　。
biàn　gèng　　wéi　yī　bú　biàn

此　話　真　，　其　必　也　變　，
cǐ　huà　zhēn　　qí　bì　yě　biàn

不　變　亦　應　為　不　變　。
bú　biàn　yì　yīng　wéi　bú　biàn

11.1.1 *King of Lanling Land*

Though Not Omnipotent but Eternal

May 9, 2020

With beginning and end,

Things all ascend and descend.

From blossom to fruit,

Nothing is absolute.

Nothing absolute per se,

It only becomes a fallacy.

To avoid the logical deficiency,

There must be an absolute entity.

Things all ever change,

It's not that strange.

Change is the only thing,

That will never change.

11.1.2　　　蘭　陵　王
lán　　líng　　wáng

上　帝　永　恒　非　萬　能
shàng　dì　yǒng　héng　fēi　wàn　néng

2020　年　5　月　9　日

此　不　變　非　變　。
cǐ　bú　biàn　fēi　biàn

其　實　為　上　天　，
qí　shí　wéi　shàng　tiān

依　次　類　算　，
yī　cì　lèi　suàn

變　更　上　天　皆　不　變　。
biàn　gèng　shàng　tiān　jiē　bú　biàn

上　天　乃　上　帝　，
shàng　tiān　nǎi　shàng　dì

勿　容　置　言　，
wù　róng　zhì　yán

上　帝　存　在　且　永　恒　。
shàng　dì　cún　zài　qiě　yǒng　héng

邏　輯　勝　雄　辯　。
luó　jí　shèng　xióng　biàn

11.1.2　*King of Lanling Land*

Though Not Omnipotent but Eternal

May 9, 2020

If only this is true,

Then I don't have a clue.

Change never changes,

It itself must change too.

Something else will also never change,

Through the basic logic of the Lagrange.

It is the absolute with nothing odd,

That's what we know as God.

There is clearly no doubt,

No matter how you argue it out.

God is existential,

And forever perpetual.

11.1.3 蘭　　陵　　王
　　　　lán　　líng　　wáng

上　帝　永　恒　非　萬　能
shàng　dì　yǒng　héng　fēi　wàn　néng

2020　年　5　月　9　日

上　帝　。　本　萬　能　。
shàng　dì　　　běn　wàn　néng

定　造　一　巨　石　，
dìng　zào　yī　jù　shí

己　不　能　肩　。
jǐ　bú　néng　jiān

既　不　肩　何　曰　萬　能　？
jì　bú　jiān　hé　yuē　wàn　néng

此　驚　天　秘　密　，
cǐ　jīng　tiān　mì　mì

突　顯　眼　前　。
tū　xiǎn　yǎn　qián

上　帝　應　有　，
shàng　dì　yīng　yǒu

且　永　恒　，　非　萬　能　。
qiě　yǒng　héng　　fēi　wàn　néng

11.1.3 *King of Lanling Land*

Though Not Omnipotent but Eternal

May 9, 2020

God is all mighty,

It creates all things and human being.

Creating a giant rock,

Should be an easy thing.

A rock so big that no one can lift,

Definitely a possibility.

If even God cannot lift,

We cannot say God is omnipotent.

Suddenly there is a secret to reveal,

God is absolute and supernal.

Like change God will never change,

Though not omnipotent but eternal.

蝶　戀　花
dié　　liàn　　huā

走　你　千　遍
zǒu　　nǐ　　qiān　　biàn

2020　年　7　月　25　日

庭　外　小　徑　走　千　遍　，
tíng　wài　xiǎo　jìng　zǒu　qiān　biàn

四　季　如　一　，　晴　雨　皆　覺　鮮　。
sì　jì　rú　yī　　qíng　yǔ　jiē　jué　xiān

此　山　彼　山　天　外　天　，
cǐ　shān　bǐ　shān　tiān　wài　tiān

良　辰　美　景　實　眼　前　。
liáng　chén　měi　jǐng　shí　yǎn　qián

城　裏　熱　鬧　城　外　羨　，
chéng　lǐ　rè　nào　chéng　wài　xiàn

城　外　寬　廣　，　城　裏　往　外　遷　。
chéng　wài　kuān　guǎng　　chéng　lǐ　wǎng　wài　qiān

天　涯　海　角　都　人　間　，
tiān　yá　hǎi　jiǎo　dōu　rén　jiān

憐　愛　珍　惜　在　身　邊　。
lián　ài　zhēn　xī　zài　shēn　biān

11.2 *Flower-Loving Butterfly*

Walk You a Thousand Times

July 25, 2020

A thousand times on the small path trail,
The four seasons have the same tale.
Rain or shine never bail,
There is always that fresh feel.

With mountain over mountain,
There is sky above sky.
The beautiful scenery at a beautiful time,
Remains within easy reach and in close sight.

Bustling city attracts outside jealousy,
Suburban spaciousness stirs envy.
Wherever living nearby or oversea,
The most cherished is too common to see.

摸　魚　兒
mō　yú　ér

自　由
zì　yóu

2020　年　9　月　18　日

問　蒼　天　，　自　由　何　物　？
wèn　cāng　tiān　　zì　yóu　hé　wù

直　教　困　屋　如　獄　。
zhí　jiāo　kùn　wū　rú　yù

漫　天　焦　味　煙　似　霧　，
màn　tiān　jiāo　wèi　yān　sì　wù

就　中　瘟　疫　猶　故　。
jiù　zhōng　wēn　yì　yóu　gù

戶　不　出　，　苟　活　居　，
hù　bú　chū　　gǒu　huó　jū

搔　頭　抓　耳　尋　思　路　。
sāo　tóu　zhuā　ěr　xún　sī　lù

微　信　恐　除　，
wēi　xìn　kǒng　chú

哪　有　顏　如　玉　？
nǎ　yǒu　yán　rú　yù

自　由　難　覓　，
zì　yóu　nán　mì

拘　中　挑　無　束　。
jū　zhōng　tiāo　wú　shù

11.3.1　*Searching for Fish with Bare Hand*

Freedom

September 18, 2020

Ask mighty God for wisdom,
What is freedom?
With burnt smoke like blume,
It's more a prison living at home.

The plague is still prevailing as it used to,
Staying indoors and living on without clue.
Stretch the brain and think it through,
With nothing interesting to do.

WeChat is to be removed,
Hard to keep interest in reading books.
Freedom is no longer an option to choose,
How do you let restrain loose?

11.3.2

摸 魚 兒
mō yú ér

自 由
zì yóu

2020 年 9 月 18 日

回 首 顧 ， 往 日 高 山 平 湖 ，
huí shǒu gù wǎng rì gāo shān píng hú

流 水 落 花 東 去 。
liú shuǐ luò huā dōng qù

雖 經 一 時 異 常 苦 ，
suī jīng yī shí yì cháng kǔ

未 必 長 久 歡 愉 。
wèi bì cháng jiǔ huān yú

儒 規 矩 ， 道 法 術 。
rú guī jǔ dào fǎ shù

威 權 中 土 贏 天 竺 。
wēi quán zhōng tǔ yíng tiān zhú

張 弛 恰 度 ，
zhāng chí qià dù

方 遊 刃 有 余 。
fāng yóu rèn yǒu yú

自 由 如 水 ，
zì yóu rú shuǐ

可 令 舟 載 覆 。
kě lìng zhōu zǎi fù

11.3.2　*Searching for Fish with Bare Hand*

Freedom

September 18, 2020

Turning head and looking back,

The ordinary things you would never track.

Like east-flowing water and falling flower,

They become things that we all lack.

One-time short-term pain,

No guarantee for long term gain.

Confucian rules and Taoist maya,

Authoritarian China wins free election India.

Right balance of ease and stress,

Lays the right way for success.

Freedom is like water,

It can flow a boat or tip it over.

燕　山　亭
yàn　shān　tíng

自 我 實 現 之 預 言
zì wǒ shí xiàn zhī yù yán

2021 年 1 月 25 日

大 凡 猶 人 ， 稱 神 選 民 ，
dà fán yóu rén chēng shén xuǎn mín

勤 奮 善 財 聰 慧 。
qín fèn shàn cái cōng huì

為 奴 埃 及 ， 羅 馬 趕 盡 ，
wéi nú āi jí luó mǎ gǎn jìn

被 擄 巴 比 倫 地 。
bèi lǔ bā bǐ lún dì

征 者 皆 逝 ，
zhēng zhě jiē shì

神 子 民 、 上 帝 寵 惜 。
shén zǐ mín shàng dì chǒng xi

今 世 ，
jīn shì

看 多 少 預 言 ， 自 我 坐 實 。
kàn duō shǎo yù yán zì wǒ zuò shí

11.4.1　*Pavilion of Mount Yan*

Self-Fulfilling Prophecy

January 25, 2021

All the Jews in the world,
Claimed themselves the Chosen of God.
Hard working and good at money,
Gravitating to what they said.

Enslaved in Egypt,
Prosecuting in Rome is no secret.
Captured in Babylon,
Gone is the conscript.

God's people, God's child.
In this world,
Many prophecies told,
Have been self-fulfilled.

11.4.2　　　燕　山　亭
　　　　　　yàn　shān　tíng

自　我　實　現　之　預　言
zì　wǒ　shí　xiàn　zhī　yù　yán

2021　年　1　月　25　日

急　品　缺　、　銀　行　潰　，
jí　pǐn　quē　　　yín　háng　kuì

夢　想　與　偏　見　，　骗　局　龐　氏　。
mèng　xiǎng　yǔ　piān　jiàn　　piàn　jú　páng　shì

言　一　是　一　，　近　朱　也　赤　，
yán　yī　shì　yī　　jìn　zhū　yě　chì

說　白　黑　亦　成　灰　。
shuō　bái　hēi　yì　chéng　huī

陰　陽　相　隨　，
yīn　yáng　xiàng　suí

何　聽　聞　、　曾　有　停　息　？
hé　tīng　wén　　céng　yǒu　tíng　xī

悖　論　，
bèi　lùn

才　自　我　實　現　反　極　。
cái　zì　wǒ　shí　xiàn　fǎn　jí

11.4.2　*Pavilion of Mount Yan*

Self-Fulfilling Prophecy

January 25, 2021

Urgent goods shortages,
Rush cashing bank collapses.
Prejudices and dreams,
The Ponzi schemes.

Saying one makes one in head,
Near crimson it turns red.
If you say there is black in white,
The white is no longer bright.

Things all have two sides,
Yin and Yang are like tides.
Only the paradox is the place,
Where the opposite of self-fulfilling resides.

知識如不能分類，則不知所知，不知所不知。其或無知，或無所不知。後者只能是上帝。

不知的已知，只管跟著感覺走，待遇到時，豁然開朗。最多不過，墙碰頭、重復投。

美防長曾說，有知的已知，那些我們知道已知道的事情。有知的未知，那些事情我們知道還不知道。但是也有不知的未知，那些我們根本不知道我們不知道。此最難。

不知之未知，是真的不知。遺憾的是，此正包含最大的知識。感於此，填《高陽臺·知識如圓》。

11.5　　　　　The Unknown Unknowns

If knowledge can't be classified, then one does not know what one knows, and one does not know what one does not know. There could be complete ignorance. Or, on the contrary, it could be the case of knowing everything. The latter can only be God.

For the unknown knowns, just proceed and follow the flow. There will be a way when you come to the front of a mountain. When the time comes, things all become clear. Or at the worst, you hit a wall and then you do it over.

Donald Rumsfeld once said, there are known knowns, there are things we know we know; there are known unknowns, there are some things we do not know; but there are also unknown unknowns—the ones we don't know we don't know, these are the hardest.

It's the unknown unknowns that make the true ignorance. Unfortunately, these are the ones that contain the greatest knowledge. Thinking it over, I started to write the poem "High Platform of Mountain South • Knowledge is like a Circle".

知　識　如　圓
zhī　shí　rú　yuán

2021　年　3　月　8　日

知　識　如　圓　，
zhī　shí　rú　yuán

規　畫　於　紙　，
guī　huà　yú　zhǐ

圈　內　僅　為　所　知　。
quān　nèi　jǐn　wéi　suǒ　zhī

立　於　圈　外　，
lì　yú　quān　wài

豁　然　知　所　不　知　，
huō　rán　zhī　suǒ　bú　zhī

格　物　致　知　更　添　知　，
gé　wù　zhì　zhī　gèng　tiān　zhī

然　久　外　、　不　知　所　知　。
rán　jiǔ　wài　　bú　zhī　suǒ　zhī

唯　圈　上　，
wéi　quān　shàng

知　己　所　知　，
zhī　jǐ　suǒ　zhī

明　己　不　知　。
míng　jǐ　bú　zhī

11.6.1　*High Platform of Mountain South*

Knowledge is like a Circle

March 8, 2020

Knowledge is like a circle,

With inside and outside but no pinnacle.

Drawing it on plain paper,

What's inside is only the known.

Stepping outside from the regular flow,

Suddenly you realize things you don't know.

Investigating the outside unknowns,

Surely enlarges the circle.

Staying outside too long,

Makes you forget what you know.

Only when you are on the circle,

You know what you know and what you don't know.

11.6.2

高陽臺
gāo yáng tái

知識如圓
zhī shí rú yuán

2021 年 3 月 8 日

拉姆斯菲爾德說，
lā mǔ sī fēi ěr dé shuō

有知的已知，
yǒu zhī de yǐ zhī

知的未知。
zhī de wèi zhī

只要是知，
zhī yào shì zhī

鬧騰不逃手指。
nào téng bú táo shǒu zhǐ

那堪不知之未知，
nà kān bú zhī zhī wèi zhī

難洞悉、令人顫栗。
nán dòng xī lìng rén chàn lì

知於心，
zhī yú xīn

泰若不知，
tài ruò bú zhī

聖人之智。
shèng rén zhī zhì

11.6.2　*High Platform of Mountain South*

Knowledge is like a Circle

March 8, 2020

Donald Rumsfeld once said,

There are known knowns,

There are known unknowns,

There are also unknown unknowns.

As long as they are known,

We can handle them on our own.

It's the unknown unknowns,

That make one really frowned.

Incomprehensible uncertainty,

Understand it by heart clearly.

Exceptionally calm with unknowns and complaints,

That is the wisdom of the saints.

留 春 令
liú chūn lìng

百 花 千 紅 來 又 去
bǎi huā qiān hóng lái yòu qù

2021 年 5 月 2 日

梅 引 春 路 ，　百 花 嬉 逐 ，
méi yǐn chūn lù　bǎi huā xī zhú

漫 天 飛 絮 。
màn tiān fēi xù

萬 紫 千 紅 滿 眼 入 ，
wàn zǐ qiān hóng mǎn yǎn rù

鶯 兒 歌 、 燕 兒 舞 。
yīng ér gē　yàn ér wǔ

東 風 催 花 卻 不 護 ，
dōng fēng cuī huā què bú hù

和 春 本 風 雨 。
hé chūn běn fēng yǔ

百 花 千 紅 來 又 去 ，
bǎi huā qiān hóng lái yòu qù

凡 世 間 、 恰 妙 處 。
fán shì jiān　qià miào chù

11.7　*Short Tune of Retaining Spring*

Spring Blossoms Come and Go

May 2, 2021

Plum leads the Spring Road,
Hundred flowers happily follow.
Frolicking with the flying catkins of willow,
Eyes full of thousands of reds and purples.

The Orioles are singing,
The swallows are dancing.
The east wind brings the blooming,
Also makes the flower petals falling.

Rain and Spring together never say no,
Flower blossoms come and go.
The world is in a full cycle,
Yin and Yang behave exactly so.

踏　莎　行
tà　　suō　　xíng

嫦　娥　觀　人　間
cháng　é　guān　rén　jiān

2021 年 6 月 5 日

繞　陽　斜　依　，
rào　yáng　xié　yī

方　得　四　季　，
fāng　dé　sì　jì

自　轉　不　歇　有　夜　日　。
zì　zhuǎn　bú　xiē　yǒu　yè　rì

奪　目　藍　星　天　上　掛　，
duó　mù　lán　xīng　tiān　shàng　guà

身　在　其　中　卻　不　知　。
shēn　zài　qí　zhōng　què　bú　zhī

文　人　騷　客　，
wén　rén　sāo　kè

儒　生　雅　士　，
rú　shēng　yǎ　shì

多　少　觀　天　管　中　窺　。
duō　shǎo　guān　tiān　guǎn　zhōng　kuī

直　教　出　匣　回　首　看　，
zhí　jiāo　chū　xiá　huí　shǒu　kàn

天　上　人　間　皆　凡　地　。
tiān　shàng　rén　jiān　jiē　fán　dì

11.8　*Treading the Sedge Path*

Heaven and Earth

June 5, 2021

Follow the Sun,
Revolve round,
Lean close and tilt,
Four seasons found.

Rotate the ground,
Blue planet of crown,
In space not knowing it,
Day and night come around.

Literati of renown,
Scholars of Confucian background,
See sky like frog in a well,
With the view field bound.

Travel far outbound,
Look back at surround,
Heaven and Earth hanging,
The world plain and sound.

人之初，性本善。人不為己，天誅地滅。此二言，聽相悖，實不違。善惡之源，不可定測。硬要分個子醜寅卯，則屬信實。信之則有，不信則無。人之為己，天經地義。此乃經濟學之根基。理性行為是平衡之必然。非理性只能暫時，與經濟學核心並無忤逆。

光照一方，猶如珠子落盤。所觸之地必受撞擊。光播四方，就像水中波紋。所到之處盡有漣漪。波粒二象，融二物於一體。性善性惡，人之為己，二者並不排斥。既有它的存在，必有它的合理性。

11.9.1　　　　The Theory of Harmonic World

In the beginning, people are inherently good. People also do things for their own good. These two statements seem to contradict each other, but they do not. The source of good or evil is indeterminate. Defining it one way or the other is more of faith. It exists when believing it. It does not when there is no belief. It is right and proper for people to act for themselves. This is the foundation of economics. Rational behavior is a necessity of equilibrium. Irrationality can only be temporary, and it is not contrary to the core of economics.

Light shining on surface is like beads falling on a plate. Where it touches, the plate will be struck. Light also propagates everywhere, like ripples in the water. There are light ripples everywhere. The nature of wave particle dual entities fuses two things into one. Neither the nature of be inherently good or bad nor doing things for themselves are mutually exclusive. When a thing exists, it must have it rationality.

和諧世界說

hé xié shì jiè shuō

諸子百家，燦爛文化。罷黜百家，獨尊儒術，似有偏差。二八原則，經驗公式，看亦是取一舍它。追遂一方，駢四儷六，然可共存，實無背謬。

世界原為和諧之世界。一切本相安無事。然縱觀歷史，朝代更替，帝國疊起，比比皆是。何也？昔研究非線性。給個時間，局於一空間，系統會進入穩定態，叫吸引子。吸引子有多個，且與起始時間相連。看來這和諧世界有許多。只要時間適恰，一個和諧世界可跳入另一個和諧世界。

11.9.2　　　　The Theory of Harmonic World

China inherits splendid culture with hundreds of philosophies. Dismissing a hundred schools of thought and revering only Confucianism seems to be biased. The twenty-eighty principle, an empirical formula, also seems to be a matter of choosing and discarding. There is however no fallacy. The pursuit of one side vs. chasing four or six sides in parallel can coexist.

The world is supposed to be a harmonious world. Everything is fine with each other. However, throughout history, dynasties come and go, and empires rise and fall, one after another, why?

I was once fortunate to study the nonlinearity in the past. Given a starting time, confined in a limited space, a system would enter a stable state, which is called attractor. There may be multiple attractors and they are directly related to the starting time. It seems that there are many attractors in this harmonious world. When the time is right, one harmonious world can jump into another harmonious world.

 西　江　月　
xī　　jiāng　　yuè

和　諧　世　界
hé　xié　shì　jiè

2021　年　7　月　10　日

光　照　如　珠　落　盤，
guāng　zhào　rú　zhū　luò　pán

四　播　似　水　波　紋，
sì　bō　sì　shuǐ　bō　wén

乍　看　不　容　兩　對　立，
zhà　kàn　bú　róng　liǎng　duì　lì

卻　是　二　象　一　身。
què　shì　èr　xiàng　yī　shēn

寰　宇　混　沌　頻　現，
huán　yǔ　hún　dùn　pín　xiàn

蓋　由　起　始　時　間，
gài　yóu　qǐ　shǐ　shí　jiān

性　善　為　己　不　排　斥，
xìng　shàn　wéi　jǐ　bú　pái　chì

和　諧　世　界　相　連。
hé　xié　shì　jiè　xiàng　lián

11.10 *Moon Over the West River*

Harmonic World

July 10, 2021

Light shining without purpose,

Like beads falling on the surface,

Propagating in all four directions,

Like the water ripples in the space.

Two different things at first glance,

Mixing them seems to have no chance.

The real nature of dual entities,

Fusing two in one would make you dance.

The world is frequently in chaos,

All depending on time advance.

Being good not opposing doing things for selves,

In harmonious worlds that are inclusive.

12 信 仰

xìn   yǎng

FAITH

清 平 樂
qīng   píng   yuè

信 仰 與 良 知
xìn yǎng yǔ liáng zhī

2020 年 2 月 15 日

奴 隸 大 赦 ，
nú lì dà shè

自 由 無 從 轍 ，
zì yóu wú cóng zhé

猶 人 篤 信 成 法 則 ，
yóu rén dǔ xìn chéng fǎ zé

始 有 聖 經 十 誡 。
shǐ yǒu shèng jīng shí jiè

中 華 文 明 不 歇 ，
zhōng huá wén míng bú xiē

從 未 青 黃 不 接 。
cóng wèi qīng huáng bú jiē

正 如 猶 人 信 念 ，
zhèng rú yóu rén xìn niàn

是 那 良 知 世 界 。
shì nà liáng zhī shì jiè

12　信　仰　FAITH

12.1　*Tunes of Purity and Peace*

Faith and Conscience

February 15, 2020

With Egyptian slave amnesty,
Freedom had no trajectory.
From the survival belief fragments,
Came the Bible's Ten Commandments.

The Chinese Civilization never stops,
As the Green and Yellow have joined in crops.
Like the Jewish beliefs and faith,
The Chinese believes in the world of conscience.

清　平　樂
qīng　píng　yuè

民　主　與　良　知
mín　zhǔ　yǔ　liáng　zhī

2020　年　2　月　15　日

民　主　何　堪　？
mín　zhǔ　hé　kān

本　因　異　議　存　，
běn　yīn　yì　yì　cún

少　數　服　從　多　數　判　，
shǎo　shù　fú　cóng　duō　shù　pàn

不　清　釀　成　混　亂　。
bú　qīng　niàng　chéng　hún　luàn

中　華　良　知　如　山　，
zhōng　huá　liáng　zhī　rú　shān

民　眾　心　中　有　算　。
mín　zhòng　xīn　zhōng　yǒu　suàn

虛　偽　炒　作　操　縱　，
xū　wěi　chǎo　zuò　cāo　zòng

人　間　良　知　盡　斷　。
rén　jiān　liáng　zhī　jìn　duàn

12.2　*Tunes of Purity and Peace*

Democracy and Conscience

February 15, 2020

How all-powerful can democracy be?

It exists because there are people who disagree.

The essence is the minority obeying the majority,

Only when there is majority and minority clarity.

Chinese conscience is as heavy as a mountain,

Common people have clear understanding.

With False hype, manipulation, and hypocrisy,

Democracy without conscience turns into mediocrity.

西 方 信 仰
xi　fāng　xìn　yǎng

2020 年 5 月 9 日

人　在　西　方　，
rén　zài　xī　fāng

隨　俗　入　鄉　，
suí　sú　rù　xiāng

耳　濡　目　染　，
ěr　rú　mù　rǎn

碰　上　信　仰　。
pèng　shàng　xìn　yǎng

信　神　無　恙　，
xìn　shén　wú　yàng

不　可　盲　仿　，
bú　kě　máng　fǎng

簡　單　推　理　，
jiǎn　dān　tuī　lǐ

盡　顯　真　相　。
jìn　xiǎn　zhēn　xiàng

請參閱第 93 篇《蘭陵王·上帝永恒非萬能》和第 143 篇《念奴嬌·
鑽木取火》。

12.3　Western Faith

May 9, 2020

Living in the west,

Follow the customs to the best.

Influenced by what you constantly perceive,

You will meet the western religious belief.

Believing in God is not problematic,

If only you do not blindly mimic.

With simple logic thinking,

The rationale all becomes compelling.

木　蘭　花　慢
mù　lán　huā　màn

初　夏　問　夜　天
chū　xià　wèn　yè　tiān

2021　年　5　月　29　日

初　夏　問　夜　天　，
chū　xià　wèn　yè　tiān

莽　星　河　，　幾　銀　漢　？
mǎng　xīng　hé　　jǐ　yín　hàn

有　限　或　無　限　？
yǒu　xiàn　huò　wú　xiàn

地　球　家　園　，　天　命　中　年　。
dì　qiú　jiā　yuán　　tiān　mìng　zhōng　nián

百　歲　時　，　何　處　遷　？
bǎi　suì　shí　　hé　chù　qiān

宜　居　地　、　遙　遙　深　空　間　，
yí　jū　dì　　yáo　yáo　shēn　kōng　jiān

沒　四　光　年　莫　言　，
méi　sì　guāng　nián　mò　yán

仙　舟　閃　渡　那　邊　？
xiān　zhōu　shǎn　dù　nà　biān

12.4.1 *Meandering Magnolia*

Ask Sky in Early Summer Night

May 29, 2021

In an early summer night,
With the sky clear and bright,
Ask the vast mighty universe,
How many galaxies shine light?

With home planet half-life in sight,
Shouldn't there be fright?
Before doomsday creeps on Earth,
Where is a new planet of twilight?

The space is never polite,
Any livable extraterrestrial site?
Far away for any traveler,
What is the vehicle when taking flight?

12.4.2

木　蘭　花　慢
mù　lán　huā　màn

初　夏　問　夜　天
chū　xià　wèn　yè　tiān

2021　年　5　月　29　日

杞　人　憂　天　昂　首　閑　，
qǐ　rén　yōu　tiān　áng　shǒu　xián

低　頭　看　眼　前　。
dī　tóu　kàn　yǎn　qián

期　遠　心　不　念　？
qī　yuǎn　xīn　bú　niàn

人　間　萬　千　，　有　限　當　然　。
rén　jiān　wàn　qiān　　yǒu　xiàn　dāng　rán

世　事　且　當　無　限　？
shì　shì　qiě　dāng　wú　xiàn

煙　火　生　、　你　我　總　陪　伴　。
yān　huǒ　shēng　　nǐ　wǒ　zǒng　péi　bàn

方　今　國　命　註　定　，
fāng　jīn　guó　mìng　zhù　dìng

問　何　無　盡　糾　纏　？
wèn　hé　wú　jìn　jiū　chán

12.4.1　*Meandering Magnolia*

Ask Sky in Early Summer Night

May 29, 2021

Thousand years of humanity in candlelight,
Earth civilizations only just ignite.
Surely there will be an end to earthly life,
Who'd care about that to ruin the appetite?

Look at the reality close and uptight,
Everyday life consumes all the might.
You and I can sit side by side,
We laugh it out with good delight.

Fate is not about wrong or right.
When a nation reaches a certain height,
Competition and collaboration go hand in hand.
Why would there be the need for entangling plight?

13 人　生

rén　shēng

LIFE

相　見　歡
xiàng　jiàn　huān

千　秋　萬　裏
qiān　qiū　wàn　lǐ

2019　年　11　月　22　日

鴻　鵠　誌　高　勝　鷹　，
hóng　hú　zhì　gāo　shèng　yīng

千　秋　輕　。
qiān　qiū　qīng

人　生　路　遙　知　力　，
rén　shēng　lù　yáo　zhī　lì

萬　裏　行　。
wàn　lǐ　xíng

勤　耕　耘　，　常　自　新　，
qín　gēng　yún　　cháng　zì　xīn

度　真　情　。
dù　zhēn　qíng

隨　心　欲　不　逾　矩　，
suí　xīn　yù　bú　yú　jǔ

看　淡　清　。
kàn　dàn　qīng

13　人　生　LIFE

13.1　*Joy of Seeing Each Other*

Thousand Autumns and Ten Thousand Miles

November 22, 2019

Swan is flying high with more aspirations than eagle,

Looking into thousand Autumns and being cool.

Only distance can distinguish trials and denials,

When traveling a journey of ten thousand miles.

Diligently cultivate with continuous renewal,

Understanding the people going through the turnstiles.

Do whatever in desire without breaking the rules,

Seeing things through without going to many schools.

浣　溪　沙
huàn　xī　shā

順　然　隨　緣
shùn　rán　suí　yuán

2020 年　4　月　8　日

人　生　年　光　易　過　，
rén　shēng　nián　guāng　yì　guò

舒　心　境　界　易　錯　。
shū　xīn　jìng　jiè　yì　cuò

順　其　然　隨　其　緣　，
shùn　qí　rán　suí　qí　yuán

無　須　刻　意　雕　琢　。
wú　xū　kè　yì　diāo　zhuó

蟪　蛄　沒　有　春　秋　，
huì　gū　méi　yǒu　chūn　qiū

朝　菌　無　需　晦　朔　。
zhāo　jūn　wú　xū　huì　shuò

13.2 *Sand Beach of Silk Washing Stream*

Follow the Fate and Go with the Flow

April 8, 2020

Life is plain to pass,
Opportunity is easy to miss.
Follow the fate as it happens,
No need for deliberate fuss.

Go with the flow,
Wherever you go.
Cicada does not know Spring or Autumn,
There is no dusk for dawn mushroom.

13.3.1 念奴嬌

niàn nú jiāo

盡誌不達無悔
jìn zhì bú dá wú huǐ

2020 年 4 月 25 日

才不及誌，　勉自力，
cái bú jí zhì　　miǎn zì lì

江水東流不息。
jiāng shuǐ dōng liú bú xī

富不支夢，　多嘗試，
fù bú zhī mèng　　duō cháng shì

機遇遇上百技。
jī yù yù shàng bǎi jì

冷暖自知，　溝坎不止，
lěng nuǎn zì zhī　　gōu kǎn bú zhǐ

順時常思逆。
shùn shí cháng sī nì

小成淡然，
xiǎo chéng dàn rán

困境切莫休遲。
kùn jìng qiē mò xiū chí

13.3.1　*Winsome Manner of Maid Niannu*

Pursuit of Great Aims with no Regret

April 25, 2020

If talent is not up to aspirations,
Strive with more perspiration.
If fortune is not enough to support dreams,
Cross more rivers and streams.

The Yangtze River flows East,
The water is forever incessant.
Opportunities always exist,
Where ambitions and skills meet.

Hold the reins of your own destiny,
Thinking in reverse in serenity.
Not just fight battles when hunky-dory,
Never let go or delay with difficulty.

13.3.2　　　　念　　奴　　嬌
　　　　　　　　niàn　　nú　　jiāo

盡　誌　不　達　無　悔
jìn　zhì　bú　dá　wú　huǐ

2020　年　4　月　25　日

彷　徨　愈　堅　誌　意　，
páng　huáng　yù　jiān　zhì　yì

勤　奮　添　智　慧　，　兼　贏　兔　龜　。
qín　fèn　tiān　zhì　huì　　jiān　yíng　tù　guī

矢　誌　不　移　，　點　滴　水　，
shǐ　zhì　bú　yí　　diǎn　dī　shuǐ

天　長　日　久　穿　石　。
tiān　cháng　rì　jiǔ　chuān　shí

終　始　不　棄　，　心　中　銘　宿　誌　，
zhōng　shǐ　bú　qì　　xīn　zhōng　míng　sù　zhì

問　心　無　愧　。
wèn　xīn　wú　kuì

灑　脫　坦　蕩　，
sǎ　tuō　tǎn　dàng

盡　誌　不　達　無　悔　。
jìn　zhì　bú　dá　wú　huǐ

13.3.2 *Winsome Manner of Maid Niannu*

Pursuit of Great Aims with no Regret

April 25, 2020

The more uncertainties fate and chance bestow,

The stronger resolve of a determined soul.

Diligence adding the wisdom of the might force,

Wins both the fast hare and the persistent tortoise.

Unwavering determination never swerves,

To one great aim that dripping water serves.

All things give way right before it,

Wearing through the stone soon or late.

Never give up with a conscience of no retreat,

Keep consistent and remain persistent.

Free and at ease, as will alone is great,

Pursuit of great aims with no regret.

13.4.1 雨霖鈴
yǔ lín líng

永 以 樂 為 鄉
yǒng yǐ lè wéi xiāng

2020 年 5 月 3 日

遠 渡 重 洋 ， 登 界 遊 方 ，
yuǎn dù chóng yáng dēng jiè yóu fāng

幾 番 滄 桑 。
jǐ fān cāng sāng

萬 卷 千 裏 書 路 ，
wàn juàn qiān lǐ shū lù

多 少 回 ， 華 年 寒 窗 。
duō shǎo huí huá nián hán chuāng

千 帆 百 橋 闖 蕩 ，
qiān fān bǎi qiáo chuǎng dàng

又 河 深 江 廣 。
yòu hé shēn jiāng guǎng

順 天 時 ， 隨 地 之 脈 ，
shùn tiān shí suí dì zhī mài

因 人 之 心 開 新 裝 。
yīn rén zhī xīn kāi xīn zhuāng

13.4.1　*Bells Ringing in the Rain*

Always Take Joy as the Hometown

May 3, 2020

Crossing the seas and oceans,

Travel to the world for varieties of notions.

Seeing through various vicissitudes,

Experience the changes of unusual magnitudes.

Read books in thousand volumes,

Walking roads of ten thousand miles.

Endure years of hard study noticed by none,

Not for the fame or the honors to be won.

Explore the world with thousand sails,

At the great timing with the right scales,

Embraced by human relation harmony,

Ringing in a new start of great enormity.

13.4.2　　　　雨　　霖　　鈴
　　　　　　　　yǔ　　lín　　líng

　　　　永　以　樂　為　鄉
　　　　yǒng　yǐ　lè　wéi　xiāng

　　2020　年　5　月　3　日

一　城　一　池　不　成　邦　，
yī　chéng　yī　chí　bú　chéng　bāng

當　是　時　，　收　復　舊　邊　疆　。
dāng　shì　shí　　shōu　fù　jiù　biān　jiāng

臥　薪　築　墙　積　糧　，
wò　xīn　zhù　qiáng　jī　liáng

會　佳　境　，　勿　須　稱　王　。
huì　jiā　jìng　　wù　xū　chēng　wáng

自　然　如　畫　，
zì　rán　rú　huà

綠　水　青　山　十　裏　花　香　。
lù　shuǐ　qīng　shān　shí　lǐ　huā　xiāng

為　無　為　無　所　不　為　，
wéi　wú　wéi　wú　suǒ　bú　wéi

永　以　樂　為　鄉　。
yǒng　yǐ　lè　wéi　xiāng

13.4.2 *Bells Ringing in the Rain*

Always Take Joy as the Hometown

May 3, 2020

One fortress, one town, one castle gate,

Not able to form a good state,

When time is right,

Reclaim the old frontier to celebrate.

Laying out plans,

Building walls and storing grains,

Wait till the situation is right.

There is no need to claim King.

It's like the picturesque nature,

With clear waters, green mountains full of flowers.

Doing nothing is for doing everything you want,

Always take joy as the hometown.

釵　頭　鳳
chāi　　tóu　　fèng

豁　達　如　海
huō　　dá　　rú　　hǎi

2020　年　5　月　16　日

少　計　量　，
shǎo　jì　liàng

多　體　諒　，
duō　tǐ　liàng

豁　達　如　海　萬　事　暢　。
huō　dá　rú　hǎi　wàn　shì　chàng

心　胸　廣　，
xīn　xiōng　guǎng

目　顏　朗　。
mù　yán　lǎng

無　爭　自　在　，
wú　zhēng　zì　zài

樂　觀　向　上　。
lè　guān　xiàng　shàng

棒　，　棒　，　棒　！
bàng　　bàng　　bàng

13.5.1 *Phoenix Hairpin*

Open-Minded like Sea

May 16, 2020

Less calculation,

More compassion,

Open-minded like sea,

All smooth things come to thee.

Broad-minded,

Pleasantly refined.

Free from being competitive,

Always remain positive.

13.5.2

釵　　頭　　鳳
chāi　　tóu　　fèng

豁　達　如　海
huō　dá　rú　hǎi

2020　年　5　月　16　日

患　得　喪　，
huàn　dé　sàng

比　短　長　，
bǐ　duǎn　cháng

咄　咄　逼　人　不　忍　讓　。
duō　duō　bī　rén　bú　rěn　ràng

狹　隘　往　，
xiá　ài　wǎng

自　私　向　。
zì　sī　xiàng

仁　惡　不　分　，
rén　è　bú　fèn

嫉　妒　張　狂　。
jí　dù　zhāng　kuáng

嗆　，　嗆　，　嗆　！
qiàng　　qiàng　　qiàng

13.5.2 *Phoenix Hairpin*

Open-Minded like Sea

May 16, 2020

Worrying about loss and gain,

Comparing the pleasure and pain,

Aggressiveness leaves with no friend,

With no willingness to Give in.

Narrow-minded,

Selfishly behaved,

Not separating ungraceful from elegant,

Be jealous and arrogant.

沁　園　春
qìn　yuán　chūn

自　若　天　仙
zì　ruò　tiān　xiān

2020 年 5 月 18 日

晝　夜　晨　夕　，　月　缺　月　圓　，
zhòu　yè　chén　xī　　　yuè　quē　yuè　yuán

無　情　當　天　。
wú　qíng　dāng　tiān

歲　月　不　留　人　，　富　貴　如　雲　，
suì　yuè　bú　liú　rén　　　fù　guì　rú　yún

名　花　猶　謝　，　繁　華　若　煙　。
míng　huā　yóu　xiè　　　fán　huá　ruò　yān

蕓　蕓　眾　生　，　茫　茫　世　間　，
yún　yún　zhòng　shēng　　　máng　máng　shì　jiān

名　利　權　勢　處　處　爭　。
míng　lì　quán　shì　chù　chù　zhēng

人　生　短　，　卻　周　而　復　始　，
rén　shēng　duǎn　　　què　zhōu　ér　fù　shǐ

天　地　循　環　？
tiān　dì　xún　huán

13.6.1　*Spring of Refreshing Garden*

Live Free as Your Heart Desires

May 18, 2020

Days and nights come with dusk and dawn,
The moon goes horned and round.
Nature is itself emotionless,
Years and months fly regardless.

Riches and honors are like weather,
The most beautiful flowers still wither.
Booming comes from endeavor,
Flourishing won't be there forever.

Every living being and every worldly thing,
Link power to influence and fame to money.
And that life's hard cling,
Becomes the endless undertaking.

13.6.2　　　　沁　園　春
　　　　　　　qìn　yuán　chūn

自　若　天　仙
zì　ruò　tiān　xiān

2020　年　5　月　18　日

執　念　物　困　繞　纏　，
zhí　niàn　wù　kùn　rào　chán

顧　彼　此　、　兩　眉　峰　不　展　。
gù　bǐ　cǐ　　liǎng　méi　fēng　bú　zhǎn

珍　惜　眼　前　人　，　不　為　物　繩　，
zhēn　xī　yǎn　qián　rén　　bú　wéi　wù　shéng

不　以　念　停　，　平　處　心　安　。
bú　yǐ　niàn　tíng　　píng　chù　xīn　ān

放　下　包　袱　，　輕　裝　簡　出　，
fàng　xià　bāo　fú　　qīng　zhuāng　jiǎn　chū

事　半　功　倍　彈　指　間　。
shì　bàn　gōng　bèi　tán　zhǐ　jiān

換　思　路　，　人　樂　心　亦　寬　，
huàn　sī　lù　　rén　lè　xīn　yì　kuān

自　若　天　仙　。
zì　ruò　tiān　xiān

13.6.2　*Spring of Refreshing Garden*

Live Free as Your Heart Desires

May 18, 2020

With obsession and material court,
It's easy to attend one thing,
But let another abort.
Juggling would make one distraught.

Treasure what you've got,
Not get materially caught.
Where one is at ease,
Where there is peace.

Pack only what the trip requires,
Take the different path that inspires.
With no thorns and briars,
Live free as your heart desires.

定 風 波
dìng fēng bō

等 閑 坐 愛 終 不 悔
děng xián zuò ài zhōng bú huǐ

2020 年 4 月 15 日

常 長 飛 行 成 慣 習 ，
cháng cháng fēi xíng chéng guàn xí

消 磨 閑 時 寫 寫 詩 。
xiāo mó xián shí xiě xiě shī

思 緒 一 出 不 易 息 ，
sī xù yī chū bú yì xī

莫 追 ，
mò zhuī

鍵 矢 一 發 難 收 拾 。
jiàn shǐ yī fā nán shōu shí

13.7.1 *Calming the Winds and Waves*

Passions Never Regret

April 15, 2020

Not that I love travel,

Economics tells where we go.

Frequent long trip becomes routine,

Writing is only just waiting.

Repetition grows a habit,

Never aim for being a poet.

Inspiration is like hot spring,

Once started, stopping is not an easy thing.

13.7.2　　　　定　風　波
　　　　　　　　dìng　fēng　bō

等　閑　坐　愛　終　不　悔
děng　xián　zuò　ài　zhōng　bú　huǐ

2020　年　4　月　15　日

疫　中　困　家　幾　多　事　？
yì　zhōng　kùn　jiā　jǐ　duō　shì

若　意　，
ruò　yì

或　多　是　少　憑　次　第　。
huò　duō　shì　shǎo　píng　cì　dì

蹉　跎　本　不　人　生　稀　，
cuō　tuó　běn　bú　rén　shēng　xī

但　遂　，
dàn　suí

等　閑　坐　愛　終　不　悔　。
děng　xián　zuò　ài　zhōng　bú　huǐ

13.7.2　*Calming the Winds and Waves*

Passions Never Regret

April 15, 2020

With the epidemic continues to roam,
Many can only work out of home.
How busy can it really be?
Depending upon the priority.

Wasting time in life is not rare,
If only there are a lot of days to spare.
Doing things over does not forget,
Passions never regret.

好書易讀，千頁亦快。好客可人，百請不來。世事相違，陰陽相隨。如願所懷，百年幾回？一壺酒，一竿身，快活如伊有幾人？

hǎo shū yì dú，qiān yè yì kuài。hǎo kè kě rén，bǎi qǐng bú lái。shì shì xiàng wéi，yīn yáng xiàng suí。rú yuàn suǒ huái，bǎi nián jǐ huí？yī hú jiǔ，yī gān shēn，kuài huó rú yī yǒu jǐ rén？

不算結束，直到結束，人生是旅程。沒有目的地，一生酸甜咸辣苦，百年亦短，一日難度。唯五味俱全，才是人生真諦。

bú suàn jié shù，zhí dào jié shù，rén shēng shì lǚ chéng。méi yǒu mù de dì，yī shēng suān tián xián là kǔ，bǎi nián yì duǎn，yī rì nán dù。wéi wǔ wèi jù quán，cái shì rén shēng zhēn dì。

觀世界，無論中西，浮生塵世，概莫能外。昔日手表縫紉機，如今私島直升飛。參差不齊，才求無止境。開心即可，自在最真。

guān shì jiè，wú lùn zhōng xī，fú shēng chén shì，gài mò néng wài。xī rì shǒu biǎo féng rèn jī，rú jīn sī dǎo zhí shēng fēi。cān cī bú qí，cái qiú wú zhǐ jìng。kāi xīn jí kě，zì zài zuì zhēn。

眾心所想，眾人所過，觀念本沒對錯，填《滿庭芳·子之歌》。

zhòng xīn suǒ xiǎng，zhòng rén suǒ guò，guān niàn běn méi duì cuò，tián《mǎn tíng fāng·zǐ zhī gē》。

13.8　　　　　The Joys of Life

A good book is easy to read, and a thousand pages can go fast. A good guest is pleasant, and the guest may not come even after a hundred times of trials of invitation. Things go together with opposite sides, Yin and Yang go hand in hand. How many times in a hundred years when things occur exactly as one wishes? How many people are there with a pot of wine, standing there alone, and having a happy life?

Not the end, until the end, life is a journey. Without a destination, life has ups and downs. For some, a hundred years is short, and for others, one day is too long. Sour, sweet, bitter, spicy and crispy, only having tasted all the five flavors of life is the true meaning of life.

Viewing the world, no matter whether it is Chinese or foreign, there is no exception to the commonality of the earthly society. Watches, bicycles, and sewing machines in the China 70's pursued articles are now met with private islands, yachts, and private jets. As long as there is wealth gap, the pursuit never ends. The essence of life is, be comfortable, be happy.

Looking at what people think, what they want, what people experience, there is no right or wrong. Thinking it over, I started to write the poem "Sweet Smell in the Whole Courtyard • Song of Masters".

滿　庭　芳
mǎn　tíng　fāng

子　之　歌
zǐ　zhi　gē

2021 年 2 月 27 日

金　子　銀　子　，　交　子　會　子　，
jīn　zǐ　yín　zǐ　　　jiāo　zǐ　huì　zǐ

寬　余　不　怕　票　子　。
kuān　yú　bú　pà　piào　zǐ

房　子　孩　子　，
fáng　zǐ　hái　zǐ

在　外　高　位　子　。
zài　wài　gāo　wèi　zǐ

妻　子　如　天　仙　子　，
qī　zǐ　rú　tiān　xiān　zǐ

人　嘖　羨　、　幸　福　日　子　。
rén　zé　xiàn　　xìng　fú　rì　zǐ

橫　豎　看　、　漢　上　驕　子　，
héng　shù　kàn　　hàn　shàng　jiāo　zǐ

瀟　灑　一　輩　子　。
xiāo　sǎ　yī　bèi　zǐ

13.9.1 *Sweet Smell in the Whole Courtyard*

Song of Masters

February 27, 2021

Gold master and silver master,

Trade master and meet master.

The abundance is not afraid of,

The paper money master.

Home master and children master,

Outside job position master,

With wife master like fairy beauty master,

People are envious of the happy days master.

Look at whichever factor,

A Han Dynasty's proud man master.

With grace and flair,

An elegant life master.

13.9.2

滿 庭 芳
mǎn tíng fāng

子 之 歌
zǐ zhī gē

2021 年 2 月 27 日

學 富 五 車 子 ，
xué fù wǔ chē zǐ

老 子 孔 子 ， 墨 子 荀 子 。
lǎo zǐ kǒng zǐ mò zǐ xún zǐ

淮 南 子 ，
huái nán zǐ

博 長 百 家 諸 子 。
bó cháng bǎi jiā zhū zǐ

隨 心 不 帶 岔 子 。
suí xīn bú dài chà zǐ

世 事 處 、 勞 謙 君 子 。
shì shì chù láo qiān jūn zǐ

惜 身 子 ， 不 鈍 腦 子 ，
xī shēn zǐ bú dùn nǎo zǐ

一 個 半 甲 子 。
yī gè bàn jiǎ zǐ

13.9.2 *Sweet Smell in the Whole Courtyard*

Song of Masters

February 27, 2021

With knowledge filling up five cars,

Understanding Kong master and Lao master,

Also knowing Mo master and Xun master,

A profound mind of learning master.

Good command of the Huai River South master,

Special skill in combining hundreds of masters.

Do things that one really desires,

Not breaking the rules that society requires.

A gentleman in handling earthly affairs,

Cherish health and excellent care,

Keep a sharp mind and good ears,

Even after a long life of ninety years.

浪　淘　沙
làng　　táo　　shā

惜　花
xī　　huā

2021 年 4 月 10 日

西　村　北　天　際　，
xī　cūn　běi　tiān　jì

郁　金　香　季　。
yù　jīn　xiāng　jì

年　年　欲　往　卻　負　期　。
nián　nián　yù　wǎng　què　fù　qī

近　水　樓　臺　猶　不　急　，
jìn　shuǐ　lóu　tái　yóu　bú　jí

待　去　才　惜　。
dài　qù　cái　xī

多　少　人　生　事　，
duō　shǎo　rén　shēng　shì

匆　匆　來　逝　。
cōng　cōng　lái　shì

過　後　始　領　真　情　意　。
guò　hòu　shǐ　lǐng　zhēn　qíng　yì

奈　有　先　知　不　錯　失　？
nài　yǒu　xiān　zhī　bú　cuò　shī

莫　言　背　時　。
mò　yán　bèi　shí

13.10　*Wave Scouring Sand*

Cherish Flowers

April 10, 2021

Over the northern horizon,
It is Seattle's tulip season.
Every year there is a plan to go,
Always miss the blossom show.

There is no hurry as it is near,
Regret no going when it is over.
Life has many things,
Come and go without warnings.

Only after it disappears,
The true appreciation begins.
There is no one who can tell future,
Do not complain about misfortune.

偶聞李春平軼事，域內外先後人生，堪值拍案驚奇。七八年，二十八歲北京青年。倜儻潦倒，卻長一洋人臉。不需護照，堂而皇之，進出北京飯店。崇洋盛時，尋與洋人搭訕，謀求國外發展。

無獨有偶，好萊塢頂級女星，年已六十又七。守寡多年，卻腰纏億貫。夜夢東方情人，年少英俊。終不能自拔，逐夢中國北京。帝國大廈般，尋那不眠之夜。改革開放初，神州大地，嫩草綠綠如茵。

13.11.1   The Tale of Chunping Li

Purely by accident, I heard the story of Chunping Li, whose life in China and America, before and after, is not short of amazing. In 1978, a twenty-eight-year-old young man from Beijing, handsome but poor, however has a face like a foreigner. Because of his look, he was able to enter the Beijing Hotel free from showing a passport, which was mandatory at that time when worshipping foreign things was rife. He frequently showed up in the hotel striking up conversations with foreigners and trying to seek foreign development opportunities.

Coincidentally, a top Hollywood actress, sixty-seven years old, widowed for many years, old money rich as a billionaire, dreamed an oriental lover, young and handsome. She could not extricate herself from the thought and decided to visit Beijing, in an Empire Building style of romantic way, hoping to find the lover from the dream. China was just starting to reform and open, with the entire land curious about anything that was coming from abroad.

13.11.2　春平軼事

chūn píng yì shì

非幹柴烈火，卻有需存求。自尊不舍，養子幹娘，輕易移民美利堅。八尺男兒，本亦心存高遠。異國他鄉處，高墻圍城外，新鮮生活不易。現實無奈，歲月無情。烹茶煮飯，揉肩捶背，待為小情人。持東方人之特有細膩，儒家文化之謙讓隱忍，蹉跎十三年。漸贏湧泉相報之心。病榻前，垂危時。婚證與遺囑同至。人民幣三百億，皆留北京人。惟情至深處，獨占意也濃。遺囑明規，不允再娶生嗣。

13.11.2　　　　　The Tale of Chunping Li

It was not like dry wood and fire, but there were needs and pursuits. Not willing to give up a man's self-esteem, taking the approach of becoming an adopted son, Chunping immigrated to America. A tall young man originally had lofty aspirations. However, fresh life in a foreign land, completely different from the one he had before, turned out to be challenging. Reality was helpless, years were ruthless. Eventually he became a little lover, making tea and cooking meals, rubbing shoulders and massaging back.

Holding the peculiar delicacy of the Asian people, the humility and forbearance of Confucianism tradition, spending thirteen years, Chunping gradually won the heart of the actress who would reward back like a never-stopping hot spring. Before the sickbed and in critical condition, the marriage certificate and the will came at the same time. The sum of RMB 30 billion was all left to the Beijing young man. However, with love to the depth, the possessive desire dominates. The will clearly stipulates that no remarriage or offspring is ever allowed.

13.11.3　春平軼事

chūn píng yì shì

攜天文數字，九一年返京。漸漸廣撒同情，處處樂善好施。譽為慈善家，深受民間贊語。如今年已七旬，慢現阿爾茨海默癥。自不是淒涼，但難繞人生輪回。有問若重來，會何抉擇？答曰寧做平常人。

xié tiān wén shù zì, jiǔ yī nián fǎn jīng. jiàn jiàn guǎng sā tóng qíng, chù chù lè shàn hǎo shī. yù wéi cí shàn jiā, shēn shòu mín jiān zàn yǔ. rú jīn nián yǐ qī xún, màn xiàn ā ěr cí hǎi mò zhèng. zì bú shì qī liáng, dàn nán rào rén shēng lún huí. yǒu wèn ruò chóng lái, huì hé jué zé? dá yuē níng zuò píng cháng rén.

春平軼事，中文多有著說，國內多有專訪。國外媒體，不見只字片語。正是九四年，二十六歲妙齡女，安娜·妮可·史密斯，嫁八十九歲大亨，約翰·豪沃得·馬歇爾。媒體如錢塘之潮，倒海而來。令人詫異。拾顎之余，頗有感慨。而填《水調歌頭·青春價幾何》。

chūn píng yì shì, zhōng wén duō yǒu zhù shuō, guó nèi duō yǒu zhuān fǎng. guó wài méi tǐ, bú jiàn zhī zì piàn yǔ. zhèng shì jiǔ sì nián, èr shí liù suì miào líng nǚ, ān nà · nī kě · shǐ mì sī, jià bā shí jiǔ suì dà hēng, yuē hàn · háo wò dé · mǎ xiē ěr. méi tǐ rú qián táng zhī cháo, dǎo hǎi ér lái. lìng rén chà yì. shí è zhī yú, pō yǒu gǎn kǎi. ér tián 《shuǐ diào gē tóu · qīng chūn jià jǐ hé》.

13.11.3   The Tale of Chunping Li

With an astronomical figure of fortune, Chunping returned to Beijing in 1991. He started to spread his wealth, showing sympathy, kindness, and benevolence everywhere, hailed as Philanthropist, deeply praised by the people. As of this writing, he is his seventies, with the symptoms of Alzheimer's disease slowing appearing. Not really desolate, he can't reincarnate in life like anyone would wish that one could. He was asked once that what he would differently if he had choice to do it over. The answer was to be an ordinary person.

There have been many reporting and sayings in Chinese and in China about Chunping's story. There have been many TV interviews as well. However, there has not been a word from foreign media. It was in 1994, twenty-six-year-old Anna Nicole Smith married eighty-nine-year-old tycoon John Howard Marshall. The media was like the tide of Qiantang, pouring from the sea. The contrast was indeed a huge surprise. While picking my fallen jaw and thinking more, I started to write the poem "Prelude to the Water Melody • The Price of Youth".

水調歌頭
shuǐ diào gē tóu

青　春　價　幾　何
qīng chūn jià jǐ hé

2021 年 10 月 15 日

問　悠　悠　蒼　天　，
wèn yōu yōu cāng tiān

青　春　價　幾　何　？
qīng chūn jià jǐ hé

多　少　挖　金　女　郎　，
duō shǎo wā jīn nǚ láng

秤　稱　鬥　量　過　。
chèng chēng dòu liàng guò

八　十　年　代　中　國　，
bā shí nián dài zhōng guó

倜　儻　潦　倒　男　兒　，
tì tǎng liáo dǎo nán ér

不　識　億　為　多　。
bú shí yì wéi duō

人　世　不　銅　計　，
rén shì bú tóng jì

如　何　知　微　碩　。
rú hé zhī wēi shuò

13.12.1　*Prelude to the Water Melody*

The Price of Youth

October 15, 2021

Ask everlasting heaven of truth,

What is the price of youth?

How many young gold diggers,

Have tried to measure and deduce?

In the 1980s of China,

An opening and embracing era,

For a handsome and poor young man,

100 million would never appear in an idea.

In this secular world of cold,

All are measured in gold.

To tell scarce from abundance,

Need to wait till things are sold.

13.12.2

水　調　歌　頭
shuǐ　diào　gē　tóu

青　春　價　幾　何
qīng　chūn　jià　jǐ　hé

2021　年　10　月　15　日

芳　華　短　，　歲　月　長　，
fāng　huá　duǎn　　suì　yuè　cháng

域　外　闊　。
yù　wài　kuò

高　墙　圍　城　，
gāo　qiáng　wéi　chéng

墙　裏　熱　鬧　墙　外　惑　。
qiáng　lǐ　rè　nào　qiáng　wài　huò

高　矮　肥　瘦　挑　個　，
gāo　ǎi　féi　shòu　tiāo　gè

富　貴　貧　賤　難　說　，
fù　guì　pín　jiàn　nán　shuō

更　陰　差　陽　錯　。
gèng　yīn　chà　yáng　cuò

順　其　然　為　福　，
shùn　qí　rán　wéi　fú

人　生　本　蹉　跎　。
rén　shēng　běn　cuō　tuó

13.12.2　*Prelude to the Water Melody*

The Price of Youth

October 15, 2021

Life is long and youth is short,

Outside world is always exotic.

Envy is like a surrounding wall,

Outsiders want in and insiders want out.

Pick a mate by a ranking score,

Hard to predict rich or poor.

Things as they are in the world,

Bad turn out would make heart sore.

Blessing is to let it be,

Mind should be open like sea.

Dull and boring and joyful and exciting,

Life is all about me being me.

玉 樓 春
yù lóu chūn

分 手
fèn shǒu

2021 年 10 月 23 日

兩　情　若　是　如　初　見　，
liǎng　qíng　ruò　shì　rú　chū　jiàn

何　有　離　散　相　不　憐　。
hé　yǒu　lí　sàn　xiàng　bú　lián

等　閑　變　卻　故　人　心　，
děng　xián　biàn　què　gù　rén　xīn

卻　道　故　人　心　易　變　。
què　dào　gù　rén　xīn　yì　biàn

千　裏　之　行　九　百　半　，
qiān　lǐ　zhī　xíng　jiǔ　bǎi　bàn

一　半　崎　嶇　一　半　坦　。
yǐ　bàn　qí　qū　yǐ　bàn　tǎn

人　生　且　長　喜　多　愁　，
rén　shēng　qiě　cháng　xǐ　duō　chóu

早　知　今　日　猶　不　怨　。
zǎo　zhī　jīn　rì　yóu　bú　yuàn

大三的女兒分手了，有感難抑。

13.13　*Spring of Jade Tower*

Separation

October 23, 2021

If it's always like when two first met,
Why would be there time to regret?
Not that it's easy to break faith,
For reasons one can change mindset.

Nine hundred miles is only halfway set,
The 2nd half of the thousand miles makes one fret.
Life is a long journey of joy and sorrow,
Knowing it earlier won't change the bet.

14 觀　世　界

guān　shì　jiè

SEE THE WORLD

玉　樓　春
yù　lóu　chūn

巴　黎　聖　母　院
bā　lí　shèng　mǔ　yuàn

2019　年　4　月　15　日

八　百　多　年　月　與　日　，
bā　bǎi　duō　nián　yuè　yǔ　rì

金　園　寶　剎　傲　巴　黎　。
jīn　yuán　bǎo　shā　ào　bā　lí

彈　指　飛　間　煙　焰　去　，
tán　zhǐ　fēi　jiān　yān　yàn　qù

燒　劫　旁　延　及　萬　裏　。
shāo　jié　páng　yán　jí　wàn　lǐ

敢　賭　未　來　三　趨　勢　，
gǎn　dǔ　wèi　lái　sān　qū　shì

聯　合　州　國　拉　美　易　。
lián　hé　zhōu　guó　lā　měi　yì

凱　撒　大　地　遍　可　蘭　，
kǎi　sā　dà　dì　biàn　kě　lán

中　央　王　國　返　盛　世　。
zhōng　yāng　wáng　guó　fǎn　shèng　shì

4 月 15 日，美國報稅截至日。巴黎聖母院大火，震驚有感。

14.1 *Spring of Jade Tower*

Notre Dame de Paris

April 15, 2019

On this money collection day of Uncle Sam,

Comes the shocking news of Notre Dame.

For eight hundred years it never gave in,

A merciless fire brings to its ruin.

Flicking flames on the prideful Paris pagoda,

Extended the ripple effect thousands of miles afar.

Lost out is the beacon icon of Maria,

Ushered in is a new unforeseen era.

In a new world of three third spheres,

First is the United States of Latinized America,

Second is the Europe full of Calipha,

And the third is the rising Middle Kingdom of China.

April 15 is America's Tax Day. It's shocking to see Notre Dame de Paris on fire. It's so prompting. I was inspired to write the poem.

滿　江　紅
mǎn　jiāng　hóng

觀　世　界
guān　shì　jiè

2019　年　9　月　1　日

爬　山　登　高　，
pá　shān　dēng　gāo

觀　世　界　、　寰　宇　蒼　蒼　。
guān　shì　jiè　　huán　yǔ　cāng　cāng

五　千　年　、　不　屈　不　饒　，
wǔ　qiān　nián　　bú　qū　bú　ráo

萬　古　存　長　。
wàn　gǔ　cún　cháng

斯　德　哥　摩　癥　侯　傷　，
sī　dé　gē　mó　zhèng　hóu　shāng

奴　化　軟　弱　致　崇　洋　。
nú　huà　ruǎn　ruò　zhì　chóng　yáng

伶　仃　洋　，
líng　dīng　yáng

有　幾　只　蒼　蠅　，
yǒu　jǐ　zhī　cāng　yíng

嗡　嗡　響　。
wēng　wēng　xiǎng

14.2.1　*Full Red River*

See the World

September 1, 2019

Climb that mountain high,

Reach up to the sky,

Seeing the present and past,

And the whole world that is so vast.

Over five thousand years,

It always preservers.

The Chinese nation,

Persists the everlasting duration.

Stockholm syndrome,

Being enslaved for too long.

A few flies in the Sea of Lingding,

Make noise by just humming.

14.2.2　　　滿　　江　　紅
　　　　　　　mǎn　　jiāng　　hóng

觀　世　界
guān　shì　jiè

2019　年　9　月　1　日

德　先　生　，　不　適　當　。
dé　xiān　shēng　　bú　shì　dāng

賽　先　生　，　大　發　揚　。
sài　xiān　shēng　　dà　fā　yáng

嘆　五　四　先　賢　，
tàn　wǔ　sì　xiān　xián

大　多　迷　茫　。
dà　duō　mí　máng

西　方　歷　史　美　化　腔　，
xī　fāng　lì　shǐ　měi　huà　qiāng

自　由　民　主　不　能　幫　。
zì　yóu　mín　zhǔ　bú　néng　bāng

到　頭　來　、　要　民　族　富　強　，
dào　tóu　lái　　yào　mín　zú　fù　qiáng

靠　把　槍　。
kào　bǎ　qiāng

14.2.2 *Full Red River*

See the World

September 1, 2019

Western democracy,

Not necessarily better than meritocracy.

Science and technology,

Only the real development key.

Pity the May Fourth pioneers,

Mostly confused in arrears.

The beautification of western history,

Never tells the medieval mystery.

Freedom and democracy can be wrong,

If people are not coming along.

To make a country prosperous and strong,

In the end, is through a gun.

東 方 人
dōng fāng rén

2019 年 11 月 11 日

臺 灣 香 港 大 陸 ，
tái wān xiāng gǎng dà lù
日 韓 朝 蒙 古 。
rì hán cháo méng gǔ
黃 皮 膚 、 域 外 人 看 ，
huáng pí fū yù wài rén kàn
只 有 東 方 人 族 。
zhī yǒu dōng fāng rén zú
東 方 血 、 源 遠 不 絕 ，
dōng fāng xuè yuán yuǎn bú jué
炎 黃 蚩 尤 嗣 無 數 。
yán huáng chī yóu sì wú shù
東 方 人 、 辱 名 蔑 稱 ，
dōng fāng rén rǔ míng miè chēng
驕 立 族 戶 。
jiāo lì zú hù

Orientals: 東方人，西方人對東亞人的蔑稱。

14.3.1 *Prelude of Crowing Warbler*

The Orientals

November 11, 2019

From Taiwan, Hong Kong, Mainland China,

Or Japan, Korea, Mongolia,

Yellow people, seen from an outsider,

Only Orientals from East Asia.

The blood of the East,

The source is distant,

The stream is endless,

And the descent is countless.

The Orientals,

In the western value fundamentals,

A stigmatized race claim,

Proudly established the name.

14.3.2　　　鶯　啼　序
　　　　　　　　yīng　tí　xù

東　方　人
dōng　fāng　rén

2019　年　11　月　11　日

西　人　憶　短　，
xī　rén　yì　duǎn

泱　泱　東　國　，
yāng　yāng　dōng　guó

僅　記　長　辮　梳　。
jǐn　jì　cháng　biàn　shū

直　裸　裸　、排　華　法　案　，
zhí　luǒ　luǒ　　pái　huá　fǎ　àn

今　人　仍　有　謀　蓄　。
jīn　rén　réng　yǒu　móu　xù

紐　約　街　、聯　合　國　前　，
niǔ　yuē　jiē　　lián　hé　guó　qián

族　內　鬥　、橫　眉　冷　目　。
zú　nèi　dòu　　héng　méi　lěng　mù

時　愚　昧　，短　視　幼　稚　，
shí　yú　mèi　　duǎn　shì　yòu　zhì

窮　途　末　路　。
qióng　tú　mò　lù

14.3.2　*Prelude of Crowing Warbler*

The Orientals

November 11, 2019

Westerners' memory does not last,

Not knowing much on the great country's past.

In the harmonic Confucian society,

The image is only the long braid of Qing Dynasty.

With no attempt to be abstract,

Came the Chinese Exclusion Act.

Even among today's Capitol Hill clans,

They still have the notorious plans.

From New York streets and the United Nations,

Infighting often happens within the East Asians.

For the short-sighted, naïve and ignorant,

There is no future and it's a dead end.

14.3.3　　　鶯　啼　序
　　　　　　yīng　tí　xù

東　方　人
dōng　fāng　rén

2019　年　11　月　11　日

西　遷　喬　移　，
xī　qiān　qiáo　yí

人　籬　下　寄　，
rén　lí　xià　jì

如　猶　人　客　居　。
rú　yóu　rén　kè　jū

削　尖　頭　、依　不　能　進　，
xuē　jiān　tóu　yī　bú　néng　jìn

儒　家　血　液　，
rú　jiā　xuè　yè

涇　渭　分　明　，
jīng　wèi　fèn　míng

歷　來　如　初　。
lì　lái　rú　chū

14.3.3　*Prelude of Crowing Warbler*

The Orientals

November 11, 2019

Immigrating to the West,
Depends on others at the best.
It's like the Jewish living as guest,
In the western land of Egypt.

Sharpen your head and still can't get in,
Confucian blood is the original sin.
This is the way it has been,
Ever since the very beginning.

14.3.4　鶯　啼　序
yīng　tí　xù

東　方　人
dōng　fāng　rén

2019　年　11　月　11　日

深　色　印　人　，
shēn　sè　yìn　rén

如　魚　得　水　，
rú　yú　dé　shuǐ

殖　民　長　久　特　征　墜　，
zhí　mín　cháng　jiǔ　tè　zhēng　zhuì

失　道　助　、　僅　邯　鄲　學　步　。
shī　dào　zhù　　jǐn　hán　dān　xué　bù

泰　山　壓　頂　，
tài　shān　yā　dǐng

方　知　己　所　不　欲　，
fāng　zhī　jǐ　suǒ　bú　yù

勿　施　他　人　訓　語　。
wù　shī　tā　rén　xùn　yǔ

14.3.4 *Prelude of Crowing Warbler*

The Orientals

November 11, 2019

Like a fish in the water,

The difference of Indians is clear.

Long colonial oppression ends in assimilation,

You lose own feature and become David's deer.

An unjust cause loses support,

Learning halfway is still short.

Until seeing the enormous magnitude,

You will suddenly change the attitude.

14.3.5

鶯　啼　序
yīng　tí　xù

東　方　人
dōng　fāng　rén

2019　年　11　月　11　日

成　者　為　王　，
chéng　zhě　wéi　wáng

敗　者　為　寇　，
bài　zhě　wéi　kòu

前　朝　遺　老　去　。
qián　cháo　yí　lǎo　qù

理　當　此　、舞　臺　讓　出　，
lǐ　dāng　cǐ　　wǔ　tái　ràng　chū

若　真　才　略　，
ruò　zhēn　cái　lüè

樹　竿　招　人　，
shù　gān　zhāo　rén

重　振　旗　鼓　。
chóng　zhèn　qí　gǔ

14.3.5 *Prelude of Crowing Warbler*

The Orientals

November 11, 2019

The winner turns the King,
The loser becomes nothing.
Gone is the previous reign,
Rightfully so, let the new stage begin.

If there is real leader talent,
Take up the giant challenge.
Erect a flag and attract people,
Turning the illegal into the legal.

14.3.6 鶯 啼 序
yīng tí xù

東 方 人
dōng fāng rén

2019 年 11 月 11 日

歷 史 傳 承 ，
lì shǐ chuán chéng

中 華 瑰 寶 ，
zhōng huá guī bǎo

安 能 說 封 建 遺 俗 ？
ān néng shuō fēng jiàn yí sú

今 世 界 、 實 不 言 而 喻 。
jīn shì jiè shí bú yán ér yù

唯 有 中 央 王 朝 ，
wéi yǒu zhōng yāng wáng cháo

世 人 面 前 ，
shì rén miàn qián

東 方 一 處 。
dōng fāng yī chù

14.3.6　*Prelude of Crowing Warbler*

The Orientals

November 11, 2019

Historical heritage,
That is what the Chinese cherish.
How can it be blemished?
That it is the feudal legacy rubbish?

In today's world, it is self-evident,
Only the Middle Kingdom of the East,
Standing alone and being confident,
Shows the world that it is magnificent.

自　由　女　神
zì　yóu　nǔ　shén

2020　年　2　月　12　日

哈　德　森　河　，　埃　利　斯　島　，
hā　dé　sēn　hé　　　āi　lì　sī　dǎo

紐　約　下　城　。
niǔ　yuē　xià　chéng

揮　手　向　移　民　，　自　由　女　神　。
huī　shǒu　xiàng　yí　mín　　zì　yóu　nǔ　shén

愛　爾　蘭　人　，　意　大　利　人　。
ài　ěr　lán　rén　　yì　dà　lì　rén

大　西　洋　岸　，　紛　來　沓　至　，
dà　xī　yáng　àn　　fēn　lái　tà　zhì

美　國　熔　爐　擬　歡　迎　。
měi　guó　róng　lú　nǐ　huān　yíng

卻　不　道　，　蜂　擁　紐　約　客　，
què　bú　dào　　fēng　yōng　niǔ　yuē　kè

族　裔　分　明　。
zú　yì　fèn　míng

14.4.1　*Spring of Refreshing Garden*

The Goddess of Liberty

February 12, 2020

Hudson River,

Meets Ellis Island,

Downtown New York,

Takes pride in lower Manhattan.

The Goddess of Liberty,

Ushered immigrants in a new society.

To the Atlantic coast, one after another,

The melting pot was seen as the future.

The Irish, and the Italians,

All welcome in battalions.

But no, the flocking New Yorkers,

Only counted the distinct newcomers.

14.4.2　　　　沁　園　春
　　　　　　　qìn　yuán　chūn

自　由　女　神
zì　yóu　nǚ　shén

2020　年　2　月　12　日

熔　爐　僅　如　小　鼎　，
róng　lú　jǐn　rú　xiǎo　dǐng

自　由　平　等　只　限　歐　人　。
zì　yóu　píng　děng　zhī　xiàn　ōu　rén

然　華　夏　文　明　，　千　年　不　停　。
rán　huá　xià　wén　míng　　qiān　nián　bú　tíng

滿　人　蒙　人　，　開　封　猶　人　。
mǎn　rén　méng　rén　　kāi　fēng　yóu　rén

和　同　共　生　，　何　須　分　清　？
hé　tóng　gòng　shēng　　hé　xū　fèn　qīng

唯　講　仁　義　禮　智　信　。
wéi　jiǎng　rén　yì　lǐ　zhì　xìn

算　如　今　，　這　天　下　熔　爐　，
suàn　rú　jīn　，　zhè　tiān　xià　róng　lú

中　華　是　真　。
zhōng　huá　shì　zhēn

14.4.2　*Spring of Refreshing Garden*

The Goddess of Liberty

February 12, 2020

The glorious melting pot,

More like a small pan,

Freedom and equality,

Only limited to the European.

The flourishing Chinese civilization,

Spans millenniums without interruption,

Melting in Manchurians, Mongolians,

And the Kaifeng Jewish descendants.

With coexistence, why let difference ensure?

If there are five cardinal virtues.

Up to now, the melting pot ideal,

China is for real.

清　平　樂
qīng　　píng　　yuè

櫻　花
yīng　　huā

2020　年　3　月　15　日

春　何　時　歸　？
chūn　hé　shí　guī

華　大　櫻　花　知　。
huá　dà　yīng　huā　zhī

乍　春　還　冬　威　州　行　，
zhà　chūn　hái　dōng　wēi　zhōu　xíng

晝　夜　已　是　兩　極　。
zhòu　yè　yǐ　shì　liǎng　jí

自　為　另　類　事　實　，
zì　wéi　lìng　lèi　shì　shí

終　來　害　人　損　己　。
zhōng　lái　hài　rén　sǔn　jǐ

阿　米　麗　卡　百　姓　，
ā　mǐ　lì　kǎ　bǎi　xìng

可　憐　大　多　被　欺　。
kě　lián　dà　duō　bèi　qī

14.5　*Tunes of Purity and Peace*

Cherry Blossoms

March 15, 2020

When will Spring return?
Go to University of Washington.
With trees not able to unlearn,
The cherry blossoming is quite stern.

Wisconsin trip in the early Spring,
Cold and warm go two extreme.
With nighttime snow,
It's daytime rain.

The alternative facts,
Behave like truth cracks.
For Americans poorly informed,
Brains are pitifully scorned.

2020　年　3　月　31　日

屏　前　冗　忙　，　飛　鳥　撞　窗　。
píng　qián　rǒng　máng　　fēi　niǎo　zhuàng　chuāng

指　止　鍵　停　，　入　長　思　量　。
zhǐ　zhǐ　jiàn　tíng　　rù　cháng　sī　liàng

庭　外　陽　光　，　疫　猶　猖　狂　。
tíng　wài　yáng　guāng　　yì　yóu　chāng　kuáng

流　言　漫　天　，　蜚　語　飛　揚　。
liú　yán　màn　tiān　　fēi　yǔ　fēi　yáng

人　心　惶　惶　，　不　來　不　往　。
rén　xīn　huáng　huáng　　bú　lái　bú　wǎng

時　間　倒　流　，　中　世　紀　教　堂　。
shí　jiān　dǎo　liú　　zhōng　shì　jì　jiāo　táng

無　煙　戰　爭　，　沒　有　刀　光　。
wú　yān　zhàn　zhēng　　méi　yǒu　dāo　guāng

不　見　敵　人　，　亦　沒　卒　將　。
bú　jiàn　dí　rén　　yì　méi　zú　jiāng

護　士　醫　生　，　徒　手　陣　上　。
hù　shì　yī　shēng　　tú　shǒu　zhèn　shàng

沒　有　輜　重　，　也　無　糧　草　。
méi　yǒu　zī　zhòng　　yě　wú　liáng　cǎo

仗　怎　麼　打　？　兵　法　在　哪　？
zhàng　zěn　me　dǎ　　bīng　fǎ　zài　nǎ

該　如　何　擋　？　未　經　之　沙　場　。
gāi　rú　hé　dǎng　　wèi　jīng　zhī　shā　chǎng

14.6.1 Long Thinking

March 31, 2020

While busy in front of computer screen,
A bird hitting the window breaks the serene.
With fingers pausing and keys stopping,
I am immersed into a long thinking.

The shining sun is transient,
And the epidemic is still rampant.
With rumors filling the whole sky,
The gossip spreads to a new high.

People are panicking,
Not coming and going nor interacting.
It's like going back in time,
Falling into the medieval paradigm.

It's a smoke-free war,
Without any sword.
Not able to see enemies,
There are no present armies.

Only nurses and doctors,
All have no armors.
There is no baggage,
Neither there is forage.

How to fight?
Where to get the strategy right?
What is the shield?
It's an unchartered battlefield.

14.6.2 長　思　量

cháng　sī　liàng

2020 年 3 月 31 日

危 機 管 理 ，　紙 上 談 兵 。
wēi jī guǎn lǐ　zhǐ shàng tán bīng

大 言 不 慚 ，　不 思 其 反 。
dà yán bú cán　bú sī qí fǎn

百 姓 之 苦 ，　或 不 在 乎 。
bǎi xìng zhī kǔ　huò bú zài hū

自 負 自 私 ，　甚 為 可 怕 。
zì fù zì sī　shèn wéi kě pà

自 私 高 位 ，　尤 為 害 大 。
zì sī gāo wèi　yóu wéi hài dà

若 加 自 戀 ，　禍 起 天 下 塌 。
ruò jiā zì liàn　huò qǐ tiān xià tā

這 是 醬 缸 ，　更 是 陷 阱 ，
zhè shì jiàng gāng　gèng shì xiàn jǐng

身 入 其 中 ，　選 擇 無 他 。
shēn rù qí zhōng　xuǎn zé wú tā

朋 友 敵 人 ，　保 守 激 進 ，
péng yǒu dí rén　bǎo shǒu jī jìn

非 此 即 彼 ，　兩 極 分 化 。
fēi cǐ jí bǐ　liǎng jí fèn huà

西 方 宗 教 ，　疑 為 權 計 ，
xī fāng zōng jiāo　yí wéi quán jì

不 得 真 諦 ，　黑 暗 中 世 紀 。
bú dé zhēn dì　hēi àn zhōng shì jì

14.6.2　Long Thinking

March 31, 2020

Crisis management savior,
Only on paper.
Never ashamed of boasting,
Ignorant of reverse thinking.

The suffering of the people,
May not be anybody's sorrow.
Selfishness is deplorable,
Pretentiousness is despicable.

Selfishness at a high position,
Extremely harmful combination.
If you add narcissist acts,
The world will collapse.

This is a sauce jar,
It is also a trap.
Once you are into it,
It will be a huge mishap.

Friend or enemy,
Agree or disagree.
Conservative or liberal,
Polarizing and confrontational.

Western religion,
A temporary expedient vision.
Not getting the true meaning.
A dark medieval feeling.

14.6.3　　　　長　　思　　量
　　　　　　　　cháng　　sī　　liàng

2020　年　3　月　31　日

寄　居　華　人　，　分　崩　離　析　。
jì　jū　huá　rén　　fèn　bēng　lí　xī

族　群　不　分　，　祖　宗　不　認　。
zú　qún　bú　fèn　　zǔ　zōng　bú　rèn

思　維　怪　異　，　人　生　所　逼　。
sī　wéi　guài　yì　　rén　shēng　suǒ　bī

此　為　秦　人　，　彼　乃　清　人　。
cǐ　wéi　qín　rén　　bǐ　nǎi　qīng　rén

西　人　眼　裏　，　只　有　華　人　。
xī　rén　yǎn　lǐ　　zhǐ　yǒu　huá　rén

損　我　害　你　，　還　不　見　解　鈴　。
sǔn　wǒ　hài　nǐ　　hái　bú　jiàn　jiě　líng

非　常　時　期　，　無　以　倫　比　。
fēi　cháng　shí　qī　　wú　yǐ　lún　bǐ

歷　史　重　演　，　悲　劇　再　現　。
lì　shǐ　chóng　yǎn　　bēi　jù　zài　xiàn

家　人　勸　說　，　洗　洗　睡　了　。
jiā　rén　quàn　shuō　　xǐ　xǐ　shuì　le

凡　夫　慮　世　，　杞　人　憂　天　。
fán　fū　lù　shì　　qǐ　rén　yōu　tiān

明　日　天　晴　，　備　好　水　瓶　。
míng　rì　tiān　qíng　　bèi　hǎo　shuǐ　píng

西　圖　登　山　，　領　略　好　風　景　。
xī　tú　dēng　shān　　lǐng　luè　hǎo　fēng　jǐng

14.6.3　Long Thinking

March 31, 2020

Sojourn oversea Chinese,
Always attempt to appease.
Not holding together as an ethnic group,
Many forget ancestry root.

Weird thinking,
Forced by making a living.
Some are called Qin people,
Some are called Qing people.

In the eyes of Westerners,
There are only Chinese.
Hurting you and hurting me,
There is no glimmer of hope that we can see.

It's an extraordinary time,
With a different paradigm.
History repeats itself,
Tragedy reappears many times.

Advised by my family,
Go to bed early.
Ordinary people's scares,
Only the sky falling fears.

It will be sunny tomorrow.
Get ready your water bottle.
Seattle mountain climbing.
There is always enjoyable scenery.

長 相 思
cháng xiàng sī

脫 鉤
tuō gōu

2020 年 8 月 7 日

心 深 處 ， 藏 垢 汙 。
xīn shēn chù　　cáng gòu wū

極 端 下 濫 不 堪 目 ，
jí duān xià làn bú kān mù

危 難 真 情 露 。
wēi nán zhēn qíng lù

朝 路 數 ， 暮 不 渡 。
zhāo lù shù　　mù bú dù

潑 皮 俗 鼠 才 誌 疏 ，
pō pí sú shǔ cái zhì shū

窮 途 多 匹 夫 。
qióng tú duō pǐ fū

14.7　*Everlasting Longing for Each Other*

Decoupling

August 7, 2020

Deep in the heart,

There is filthy dirt.

Extreme gimmicks,

Only from lunatics.

In time of crisis,

True emotion rises.

Moves on the morning side,

Do not pass the evening light.

Cheeky nipper,

Vulgar rat.

Incapable in dead end,

Ugliness of ignorant brat.

咨 逍 遙
zi   xiāo   yáo

遏 製
è   zhì

2020 年 9 月 5 日

坦 克 飛 機 ，　依 賴 滾 珠 科 技 。
tǎn kè fēi jī   yī lài gǔn zhū kē jì

二 戰 時 、　竟 斷 供 給 。
èr zhàn shí   jìng duàn gòng jǐ

日 爾 曼 人 ，　並 非 等 閑 輩 。
rì ěr màn rén   bìng fēi děng xián bèi

抵 遏 製 、　智 高 超 逸 有 致 。
dǐ è zhì   zhì gāo chāo yì yǒu zhì

兩 雄 今 逐 ，　盎 盂 相 擊 。
liǎng xióng jīn zhú   àng yú xiàng jī

東 方 族 、　登 峰 造 極 。
dōng fāng zú   dēng fēng zào jí

禁 南 換 北 ，　限 東 而 出 西 。
jìn nán huàn běi   xiàn dōng ér chū xī

超 級 帝 ，　切 莫 後 悔 莫 及 。
chāo jí dì   qiē mò hòu huǐ mò jí

美國《國家利益》雜誌，2020 年 8 月 30 日文章 "為什麼特朗普的華為製裁可能反噬？" 讀後有感，填此詞。

14.8 *Acclaiming the Leisure Manner*
Containment

September 5, 2020

World War II tank,
Old airplane.
Without ball bearing,
There would be no war machine.

In critical war time,
The established cut bearing supply.
The rising Germany,
People of no ordinary.

Resisting containment,
With wisdom and savvy.
Negating the sanction,
With stronger war strategy.

Today's two powers,
Fiercely competing.
People of the East,
Reaching peak of manufacturing.

Sanctioning one thing.
They would clone,
Controlling another.
They will have their own,

Until a giant has slowly grown,
On the containment you have thrown.
The things you regret.
You wish you would have known.

永　　遇　　樂
yǒng　　yù　　lè

大　浪　淘　沙
dà　làng　táo　shā

2020　年　9　月　12　日

阿　米　麗　卡　，　　冠　狀　兇　煞　，
ā　mǐ　lì　kǎ　　　guàn　zhuàng　xiōng　shà

久　疲　不　眨　。
jiǔ　pí　bú　zhǎ

晨　霧　彌　漫　，　　推　門　細　察　，
chén　wù　mí　màn　　tuī　mén　xì　chá

勝　北　京　黃　沙　。
shèng　běi　jīng　huáng　shā

西　岸　上　下　，　　遮　天　蔽　日　，
xī　àn　shàng　xià　　zhē　tiān　bì　rì

易　染　鼻　塞　喉　啞　。
yì　rǎn　bí　sāi　hóu　yǎ

問　蒼　天　，　　奸　佞　當　道　，
wèn　cāng　tiān　　jiān　nìng　dāng　dào

情　何　雪　上　霜　加　？
qíng　hé　xuě　shàng　shuāng　jiā

2020 年 9 月 11 日，紐約恐怖襲擊 19 年。突聞白宮支持微信製裁簽名破 10 萬名。正逢西岸山火肆虐。有感疫情、山火和簽名，填此詞。

14.9.1   *Where it Forever Meets Glee*

Great Waves Sweeping Away Sand

September 12, 2020

America that used to be dynamic,

Mired in the ferocious pandemic.

With the fatigue kicking in,

Still would not let up the discipline.

The morning mist fills the air,

Open the door and examine with care.

Worse than Beijing's sandstorm,

The wildfire comes in a unique form.

Up and down the west coast,

The sky covering smoke is so gross.

Disasters seldom come alone,

Nose and throat can be easily blown.

Ask the heaven,

With bad one in charge is given,

And north wind continues to blow,

Why would add frost to the snow?

14.9.2　　　　永　遇　樂
　　　　　　　yǒng　yù　lè

大　浪　淘　沙
dà　làng　táo　shā

2020　年　9　月　12　日

泱　泱　大　國　，　炎　黃　遊　子　，
yāng　yāng　dà　guó　　yán　huáng　yóu　zǐ

才　得　五　百　萬　寡　。
cái　dé　wǔ　bǎi　wàn　guǎ

千　古　中　華　，　萬　臭　敗　類　，
qiān　gǔ　zhōng　huá　　wàn　chòu　bài　lèi

多　層　出　不　乏　。
duō　céng　chū　bú　fá

蚊　蠅　鼠　蟑　，　跳　梁　小　醜　，
wén　yíng　shǔ　zhāng　　tiào　liáng　xiǎo　chǒu

不　經　風　吹　雨　打　。
bú　jīng　fēng　chuī　yǔ　dǎ

長　歲　月　，　大　浪　淘　沙　，
cháng　suì　yuè　　dà　làng　táo　shā

砥　柱　峻　拔　。
dǐ　zhù　jūn　bá

14.9.2 *Where it Forever Meets Glee*

Great Waves Sweeping Away Sand

September 12, 2020

In the great country of America,
The wanders from old and new China,
Coast to coast and upper to lower,
Only five millions in number.

Thousands of years of Chinese history,
There is always treachery.
One after another, stinky scum,
Again and again, bum after bum.

Mosquitoes and flies,
Cockroaches and mice,
Clowns jumping beams,
Washed away in streams.

With rain and wind,
Long years and months behind,
Big waves sweeping away sand,
Only the mainstays still stand.

水 月 鏡 花
shuǐ yuè jìng huā

2020 年 9 月 26 日

《經濟學人》論評，
jīng jì xué rén   lùn píng
旁觀退聽英人清。
páng guān tuì tīng yīng rén qīng
選舉政治，無所不極，
xuǎn jǔ zhèng zhì   wú suǒ bú jí
慆慆私心。
tāo tāo sī xīn

臺灣香港，新疆西藏，
tái wān xiāng gǎng   xīn jiāng xī zàng
抖音微信。
dǒu yīn wēi xìn
信手捻來成，圍堵中國，
xìn shǒu niǎn lái chéng   wéi dǔ zhōng guó
美政客，隨點兵。
měi zhèng kè   suí diǎn bīng

適逢選舉峰至，讀《經濟學人》短文《中國經濟模式：重造國家資
本主義》，有感填詞。

14.10.1 *Water Dragon Chant*

Water Moon and Mirror Flower

September 26, 2020

An Economist article,

Shows what is not rhetorical.

The British's cunning and subtlety,

Allow them to understand with clarity.

Election politics,

Everything to use as tricks.

Normal people are helpless,

Seeing the completely bare selfishness.

Taiwan, Hong Kong, Xinjiang and Tibet,

TikTok and WeChat.

Anything handy for the containment,

US politicians will use them for own benefit.

It's America's election season. After reading the article "The Chinese Economic Model: Xi Jinping is reinventing state capitalism. Don't underestimate it.", I started writing this poem.

14.10.2

水 龍 吟
shuǐ lóng yín

水 月 鏡 花
shuǐ yuè jìng huā

2020 年 9 月 26 日

中 國 模 式 創 新 ，
zhōng guó mó shì chuàng xīn

新 製 造 避 重 就 輕 。
xīn zhì zào bì zhòng jiù qīng

國 家 資 本 ， 内 外 循 環 ，
guó jiā zī běn nèi wài xún huán

西 方 震 驚 。
xī fāng zhèn jīng

卅 年 假 定 ， 竭 力 遏 製 ，
sà nián jiǎ dìng jié lì è zhì

大 廈 必 傾 。
dà shà bì qīng

一 廂 願 ， 水 月 鏡 花 ，
yī xiāng yuàn shuǐ yuè jìng huā

不 過 井 中 窺 星 。
bú guò jǐng zhōng kuī xīng

14.10.2　*Water Dragon Chant*

Water Moon and Mirror Flower

September 26, 2020

China's new model exploration,

With the manufacturing innovation.

No more national capital public declaration,

Diligent in internal and external circulation.

It's a thirty-year assumption,

The containment strategy for a long duration.

If maintaining a separation wall,

The non-American model will fall.

The outcome to the West is shocking,

It's all wishful thinking.

Like water moon and mirror flower,

Peeping the sky from the bottom of a well.

念　奴　嬌
niàn　nú　jiāo

美　國　選　舉
měi　guó　xuǎn　jǔ

2020　年　10　月　31　日

四　年　輪　歸　，
sì　nián　lún　guī

選　舉　人　，　貴　賤　貧　富　不　欺　。
xuǎn　jǔ　rén　　guì　jiàn　pín　fù　bú　qī

多　數　亦　敗　少　數　贏　，
duō　shù　yì　bài　shǎo　shù　yíng

只　分　兩　洋　中　西　。
zhī　fèn　liǎng　yáng　zhōng　xī

樓　臺　館　榭　，
lóu　tái　guǎn　xiè

保　守　激　進　，
bǎo　shǒu　jī　jìn

人　間　百　态　披　。
rén　jiān　bǎi　tài　pī

自　由　機　製　，
zì　yóu　jī　zhì

曾　引　多　少　慕　視　。
céng　yǐn　duō　shǎo　mù　shì

選舉：2020 年 11 月 3 日是美國四年一度的總統選舉日。

14.11.1　*Winsome Manner of Maid Niannu*

American Elections

October 31, 2020

Four years of a cycle,

Voters' right is equal.

Rich or poor,

Lower or noble.

The majority still loses,

The minority also wins.

The difference is middle west,

Versus coast to coast.

Platform and stadium,

Conservatism or liberalism.

Magnificence and ugliness in every form,

The once admired freedom mechanism.

It's America's election season. After reading the article "The Chinese Economic Model: Xi Jinping is reinventing state capitalism. Don't underestimate it.", I started writing this poem.

14.11.2

念　　奴　　嬌
niàn　　nú　　jiāo

美　國　選　舉
měi　guó　xuǎn　jǔ

2020　年　10　月　31　日

而　今　囫　圇　口　齒　，
ér　jīn　hú　lún　kǒu　chǐ

無　衣　皇　帝　，
wú　yī　huáng　dì

選　他　人　如　棄　。
xuǎn　tā　rén　rú　qì

安　得　倚　天　揮　長　劍　？
ān　dé　yǐ　tiān　huī　cháng　jiàn

劈　這　腐　臭　掩　鼻　。
pī　zhè　fǔ　chòu　yǎn　bí

民　主　世　界　，　選　票　遊　戲　，
mín　zhǔ　shì　jiè　　xuǎn　piào　yóu　xì

僅　剩　填　與　誰　？
jǐn　shèng　tián　yǔ　shuí

太　平　盛　世　，
tài　píng　shèng　shì

該　回　東　國　故　地　。
gāi　huí　dōng　guó　gù　dì

14.11.2　*Winsome Manner of Maid Niannu*

American Elections

October 31, 2020

Now with words swallowed in mouth,
And the emperor without cloth.
From east to west and north to south,
American people have no good choice.

Wish to wield a long sword,
Chop up this rancid hoard.
In this democratic world,
All we have is the ballot game board?

Peace and opportunity,
Bustle and prosperity.
Isn't time to look at the East?
Find out alternatives for the least.

木　蘭　香
mù　　lán　　xiāng

無　中　生　有
wú　zhōng　shēng　yǒu

2020 年 11 月 20 日

無　中　生　有　。
wú　zhōng　shēng　yǒu

萬　物　陰　陽　二　儀　守　。
wàn　wù　yīn　yáng　èr　yí　shǒu

常　異　不　分　。
cháng　yì　bú　fèn

指　鹿　為　馬　抹　脂　粉　。
zhǐ　lù　wéi　mǎ　mò　zhī　fěn

有　目　皆　睹　。
yǒu　mù　jiē　dǔ

邪　惡　正　義　同　屋　住　。
xié　è　zhèng　yì　tóng　wū　zhù

成　王　敗　寇　。
chéng　wáng　bài　kòu

留　與　後　人　論　頌　詬　。
liú　yǔ　hòu　rén　lùn　sòng　gòu

14.12　*Magnolia Fragrance*

Something Out of Nothing

November 20, 2020

Something out of nothing,

Two sides are always in everything.

Mixing normal with odd,

Right and wrong become flawed.

We do not have to assume,

Evil and justice live in the same room.

Loser is nothing and winner takes the reign,

History is left to others to praise or disdain.

見 怪 不 怪
jiàn guài bú guài

2020 年 11 月 20 日

見 怪 不 怪 。
jiàn guài bú guài

直 視 異 類 從 容 在 。
zhí shì yì lèi cóng róng zài

清 人 長 辮 。
qīng rén cháng biàn

北 美 華 工 習 為 然 。
běi měi huá gōng xí wéi rán

醜 陋 當 家 。
chǒu lòu dāng jiā

邪 惡 亦 可 成 偉 大 。
xié è yì kě chéng wěi dà

自 由 博 愛 。
zì yóu bó ài

遠 遜 李 耳 紫 氣 來 。
yuǎn xùn lǐ ěr zǐ qì lái

14.13　*Magnolia Fragrance*

The Unusual is Usual

November 20, 2020

The unusual is usual,

Look straight into the odd and remain cool.

Qing people have long braids,

Chinese in America live in dark shades.

Ugly ones are in charge,

Evil is bound to enlarge.

Freedom and fraternity,

Far inferior to Lao Zi's philosophy.

滿　江　紅
mǎn　jiāng　hóng

中　美　對　話
zhōng měi　duì　huà

2021　年　3　月　20　日

邊　陲　僻　角　，
biān chuí pì jiǎo

冰　雪　地　、　春　不　屑　早　。
bīng xuě dì　chūn bú xiè zǎo

頂　寒　嘯　、　冷　易　無　情　，
dǐng hán xiào　lěng yì wú qíng

橫　眉　互　道　。
héng méi hù dào

無　情　不　覺　天　不　老　，
wú qíng bú jiào tiān bú lǎo

相　約　必　是　有　情　到　。
xiàng yuē bì shì yǒu qíng dào

算　世　間　、　有　情　多　難　逃　，
suàn shì jiān　yǒu qíng duō nán táo

無　情　少　。
wú qíng shǎo

中美阿拉斯加的安格瑞奇對話。唇槍舌劍，互不相讓。驕傲的帝國第一次感受到崛起大國的真正挑戰。或是民主的困惑，或是疫情的挫傷。模式的挑戰才剛剛開始。有感填詞。

14.14.1　*Full Red River*

The Anchorage Dialogue

March 20, 2021

In a remote corner,

Along the faraway border.

The land of ice and snow,

Spring disdains to go.

The frigid wind howls,

Everything is cold.

The emotionless mood,

Comes with bitter eyebrows.

The emotionless does not feel,

That the sky does not get old.

With an appointment to meet,

There must be some emotion heat.

In this world that we all share,

Emotion is hard to spare.

Even for country-to-country affair,

The emotionless is very rare.

14.14.2

满　　江　　红
mǎn　　jiāng　　hóng

中　美　對　話
zhōng　měi　duì　huà

2021　年　3　月　20　日

天　遠　高　，　寥　廓　眺　。
tiān　yuǎn　gāo　　liáo　kuò　tiào

滾　寰　塵　，　浩　蕩　潮　。
gǔn　huán　chén　　hào　dàng　cháo

百　川　水　烹　茶　，
bǎi　chuān　shuǐ　pēng　chá

不　供　東　消　。
bú　gòng　dōng　xiāo

日　月　同　天　不　同　晝　，
rì　yuè　tóng　tiān　bú　tóng　zhòu

瀚　海　為　湖　微　驚　濤　。
hàn　hǎi　wéi　hú　wēi　jīng　tāo

待　回　眸　、　不　贏　依　融　他　，
dài　huí　móu　　bú　yíng　yī　róng　tā

又　年　少　。
yòu　nián　shào

14.14.2 *Full Red River*

The Anchorage Dialogue

March 20, 2021

The sky is far and high,

Overlooking the expanse in sight.

Rolling worldly dust,

In a vast and mighty tide.

Scoop ladles of water,

From hundreds of rivers.

Boiling it to make tea,

Not enough for the people of the East.

The sun and the moon,

Share the same commune.

With day and night,

They come on the opposite side.

The Pacific is only a lake,

Waves can't cause a big quake.

Join them if you could not win,

You will realize it's a great thing.

訴　衷　情
sù　zhōng　qíng

秦　人　風　骨
qín　rén　fēng　gǔ

2021　年　3　月　27　日

崛　起　東　方　引　人　妒　，
jué　qǐ　dōng　fāng　yǐn　rén　dù

落　日　帝　國　怵　。
luò　rì　dì　guó　chù

不　是　冠　狀　病　毒　，
bú　shì　guàn　zhuàng　bìng　dú

更　非　千　年　儒　。
gèng　fēi　qiān　nián　rú

大　熔　爐　，　亦　吾　土　，
dà　róng　lú　　yì　wú　tǔ

當　吼　怒　。
dāng　hǒu　nù

攜　弓　帶　弩　，　抗　鬥　老　嫗　，
xié　gōng　dài　nǔ　　kàng　dòu　lǎo　yù

秦　人　風　骨　。
qín　rén　fēng　gǔ

野蠻鼠輩，阿米麗卡，遍地都是。專挑東方人，趁人不備偷襲。舊金山，七十五歲老人，謝蕭珍，奮起反擊，三十八歲高大白人男人，躺上擔架，進院就醫。

14.15　*Love Reminiscences*

Qin People Have Strong Character

March 27, 2021

The rise of the East makes people envy,

The declining empire feels panicky.

It's not the wide spreading Coronavirus,

Neither the millenniums of Confucius.

The big melting pot is also my land,

Together we shall roar and stand.

Like the old lady fighting the hate predator,

Qin people have strong character.

There are savage rats all over America. It is coward to pick the Orientals and attach them when they are not prepared. In San Francisco, Xiaozhen Xie, a 75-year-old lady fought back. A 38-year-old tall while man was beaten by the self-defense lady and went to hospital for medical treatment.

山 坡 羊
shān　pō　yáng

蟄 居 流 年
zhé　jū　liú　nián

2021 年 5 月 22 日

南 來 北 還 ，
nán　lái　běi　hái

穿 雲 越 山 ，
chuān　yún　yuè　shān

憶 往 昔 馳 騁 開 顏 。
yì　wǎng　xī　chí　chěng　kāi　yán

滑 鼠 鍵 ，
huá　shǔ　jiàn

網 屏 前 ，
wǎng　píng　qián

自 遨 遊 虛 擬 人 間 ，
zì　áo　yóu　xū　nǐ　rén　jiān

視 音 信 蟄 居 流 年 。
shì　yīn　xìn　zhé　jū　liú　nián

疫 ， 墮 深 淵 。
yì　　duò　shēn　yuān

苗 ， 曙 光 現 。
miáo　　shǔ　guāng　xiàn

14.16　*Hillside Sheep*

Seclusion Year Flowing Like Water

May 22, 2021

It's north and south, Its' west and east,
Traveling from coast to coast.
Crossing oceans not stranded,
Freedom was once taken for granted.

Sliding the mouse scroll wheel,
Brings a world a computer would reveal,
Roaming the virtual space with fingertips,
Even if the outside is in apocalypse.

The seclusion living flows like water,
Video and audio sustain a survivor.
Epidemic lets world fall into the abyss,
Vaccine shows the dawn of the bliss.

喜遷鶯
xǐ　qiān　yīng

資本逐利
zī　běn　zhú　lì

2021 年 7 月 4 日

紅脖子，鐵锈帶。
hóng bó zǐ，tiě xiù dài。

三十年停擺。
sān shí nián tíng bǎi。

中產世界絕望海。
zhōng chǎn shì jiè jué wàng hǎi。

短視政客害。
duǎn shì zhèng kè hài。

削軍支，自貿開。
xuē jūn zhī，zì mào kāi。

趁今猶領一代。
chèn jīn yóu lǐng yī dài。

重整產業資本來。
chóng zhěng chǎn yè zī běn lái。

定換骨脫胎。
dìng huàn gǔ tuō tāi。

14.17 *Happy as a Migrating Warbler*

Capital Chasing Profit

July 4, 2021

Red necks, and rust belt population,
Thirty years of stagnation,
The middle class is in a sea of desperation.
All by the short-sighted politicians.

Repurpose military expenses and open trade,
Let the advanced fields to be great.
Bring capital back with industry restructure,
Should be reborn with the winning culture.

民者，庶民也，乃非官。而官
者，非民也，握資源分配權。官可
變為民，民可轉為官。中華民主概
念，長闊久遠。所謂民為貴，社稷
次之，君為輕；得民心者得天下；
王侯將相寧有種乎；皆民主觀念終
極體現。

　　希臘、羅馬傳承之文明，民乃
選民，具抉擇之權。單個選民，影
響甚微。惟統計上才彰顯抉擇之意
義。所謂民主，不過是少數服從多
數。若不存多數，抉擇失去意義。
五十對五十，民主走入陷阱。

14.18.1 The Pitfalls of Democracy

The average people are common people, who are not officials. The officials are not the common people since they hold the authority to allocate resources. Officials can become common people, and common people can become officials. The concept of Chinese democracy has a long history. The paradigm that common people are precious, the country is second, and the King is last has been in Chinese philosophy for thousands of years. Those who win the support of common people win the world. There is another paradigm that Kings, Princes, Prime Ministers are not naturally born. These are the ultimate embodiment of the concept of Chinese democracy.

In the civilizations inherited from Greece and Rome, the people are the voters and have the right to choose. Individual voters have limited influence. Only in the statistical sense, can the significance of choice be highlighted. The so-called democracy is nothing more than the subordination of the minority to the majority. If there is no majority, the choice is meaningless. Fifty to fifty, democracy is in a trap.

14.18.2 過民論

guò mín lùn

文明之先進，取決資源利用之效率。而資源分配程序決定其效率之高低。選舉流程，如有絕對多少數，效率甚高，惟自由選舉鮮能達共識。威權专斷，若是精英，效率亦甚高，然昏庸需長久方能匡正。統治術，象三十六行，應有专業技能。精英管理才是最佳方式。歷史有頗多印正。羅馬帝國元老院精英；華夏文明辅佐體系；新加坡世襲民主；莫不是精英专業之範例。當今鼎盛帝國實為精英統治，非五十一對四十九之慘贏。

14.18.2   The Pitfalls of Democracy

The advancement of civilization depends on the efficiency of resource utilization. The resource allocation procedure determines its efficiency. The election process, if there is an absolute majority, is very efficient. However, free elections can rarely reach consensus. Authoritarian methodology, if it is coming from an elite, it is also very efficient. However, it takes a long time to correct individual misgivings.

The art of ruling, like the thirty-six skills and professions, should have its own professional skill. Elite professional management is the best way. History has a lot of proofs. The elite senate of the Roman Empire, the emperor and chancellor system of the Chinese civilization, the hereditary democracy in Singapore, are all examples of the elite specialty. Today's prosperous empires are ruled by elites, not by 51 to 49 free elections.

14.18.3　　過民論

guò　mín　lùn

民主非讓民做主，應是讓民成主。自由選舉是短民主，常四年。威權專斷是長民主，達二百五十年。短民主如過山車，忽上忽下。長民主如平流江河，連延不斷。精英民主，取各精華，方可成就民主之高效。不間斷、五千年，不才是民主之經典？

14.18.3   The Pitfalls of Democracy

Democracy is not to allow the common people to be the master. Rather it should let the common people become the masters. Free elections are short-term democracy, often in a four-year cycle. Authoritarianism is long term democracy; it happens over 250 years. Short term democracy is like a roller coaster, up and down. Long term democracy is like a river flowing smoothly and continuously. The elite democracy takes advantage of both worlds and can achieve the highest efficiency of democracy. Five thousand years of civilization without interruption, isn't that the classic model of democracy?

浪淘沙令
làng táo shā lìng

迷失的民主
mí shī de mín zhǔ

2021 年 7 月 17 日

五千年中華，辅佐佳話。
wǔ qiān nián zhōng huá　fǔ zuǒ jiā huà

得民心者得天下。
dé mín xīn zhě dé tiān xià

舉手定奪源希臘，
jǔ shǒu dìng duó yuán xī là

多數當家。
duō shù dāng jiā

待不分眾寡，民主如麻。
dài bú fèn zhòng guǎ　mín zhǔ rú má

卓越文明效為大。
zhuó yuè wén míng xiào wéi dà

讓民成主勝其它，
ràng mín chéng zhǔ shèng qí tā

精英才達。
jīng yīng cái dá

14.19　*Short Tune of Wave Scouring Sand*

The Lost Democracy

July 17, 2021

Five thousand years of China,

Great system of emperor and chancellor.

Winning the heart of the common people,

Will eventually win the world.

Free election comes from Greece,

Only with majority is there peace.

If there is no majority clarity,

Democracy will be in calamity.

Great civilization has great efficiency,

Letting people become masters is the priority.

Self-correction and continuity,

Only the moral elite is the best democracy.

新 風 賦
xīn　fēng　fù

和風化雨，潤土滋物，生機盎
hé fēng huà yǔ， rùn tǔ zī wù， shēng jī àng

然不艾。奧運弄潮，中華煦風，吹
rán bú ài。 ào yùn nòng cháo， zhōng huá xù fēng， chuī

拂宇內海外。優秀華夏兒女，遊泳
fú yǔ nèi hǎi wài。 yōu xiù huá xià ér nǚ， yóu yǒng

與西人拼，賽跑與非人比，贏得多
yǔ xī rén pīn， sài pǎo yǔ fēi rén bǐ， yíng dé duō

少金牌。百倍的努力，巧用的科技
shǎo jīn pái。 bǎi bèi de nǔ lì， qiǎo yòng de kē jì

，一次次的見證，彰顯世界舞臺。
yī cì cì de jiàn zhèng， zhāng xiǎn shì jiè wǔ tái。

不公平的競技場，話語規則在
bú gōng píng de jìng jì chǎng， huà yǔ guī zé zài

西方。自稱扶病，實為药幌。不只
xī fāng。 zì chēng fú bìng， shí wéi yào huǎng。 bú zhī

是東國孫楊。更可憐俄羅斯，被人
shì dōng guó sūn yáng。 gèng kě lián é luó sī， bèi rén

玩於手掌。幾百年來，西方枷鎖，
wán yú shǒu zhǎng。 jǐ bǎi nián lái， xī fāng jiā suǒ，

套在世人身上。印第安人種族屠戮
tào zài shì rén shēn shàng。 yìn dì ān rén zhǒng zú tú lù

，阿拉伯人辜死沙場。赤裸裸的排
ā lā bó rén gū sǐ shā chǎng。 chì luǒ luǒ de pái

華法案。哪個不是野蠻的篇章？
huá fǎ àn。 nǎ gè bú shì yě mán de piān zhāng

14.20.1   Ode to the New Breeze

Warm wind brings the spring rain, moistening soil and nourishing all things, full of vitality. The Olympian trend-setter, the new breeze of China, blows in the world and abroad. The excellent Chinese men and women, competing with Westerners in swimming, racing with Africans in tracks and fields, have won numerous gold medals. Hundred times of more efforts, skillful use of science and technology, witness one after another, time and time again, have highlighted on the world stage.

Unfair sports arenas have the discourse rules in the West. Claiming sick is actually a coverup for drug. It is not just Yang Sun from China, more pitiful is Russia, being played in the palms of the western hands. For hundreds of years, the Western shackles have been put on the world. The American Indians got slaughtered. The Arabs died on the battlefields. And there was a specific bill for Chinese Exclusion Act. Which of these is not a savage chapter?

14.20.2　新風賦
xīn fēng fù

原諒那些獨運輪，因他們不知
。自族的反對是禁足，西方的支持
是捆綁。受壓迫的海外炎黃子孫，
看不到翻身，只是屈從適應。只有
中華兒女的自強不息，浴火重生、
百煉更堅的華夏文明，才能造就己
所不欲、勿施於人的文明社會。
體賽的宗教慶典，間斷千年，
於西方鼎盛時重現。納長采益，見
賢思齊，本亦中華思維。韜光養晦
，不近眼前利益。勤勞苦心，放遠
長累厚積。禮儀之邦，比賽第二，
友誼第一。東方觀念，耳目一新。

14.20.2   Ode to the New Breeze

Forgive those China opposition activists because they do not know. The objection of the own China nation is only travel ban. The support of the West is shackle and chain. The oppressed overseas Chinese, unable to see a turnaround, just succumbed to adaption. Only through the continuous self-improvement of the Chinese people, the rebirth, and the strengthening of the Chinese civilization, can we create a civilized society that we will realize the Confucius value of if you do not want it, do not do it to others.

The Olympics was originated in Greece as a religious celebration of sports competition. It was interrupted for thousands of years and reappeared at the peak time of the West. It is a Chinese philosophy to align self with the common good and accept the advantages that would provide benefits. It is a Chinese strategy to hide one's strength and bide one's time, not to focus on the short-term interests. Hardworking and painstaking results in long-term accumulation. Confucius emphasizes a state of etiquette, second in competition and first in friendship. The Oriental concept is refreshing.

14.20.3　新風賦

xīn fēng fù

野蠻終將讓位文明，落後必退歷史舞臺。獵蕙草，離秦蘅，概辛夷，被荑楊，蕭條眾芳。乃得為華夏之風。辦奧運，控瘟疫，創奇跡。宛若緣太山之阿，舞於松柏之間。清清涼涼，愈病析酲，發明耳目，寧體便人。此謂東方之雄風。

420

14.20.3　　　　Ode to the New Breeze

Barbarism will eventually give way to civilization, and backwardness will retreat from the stage of history.　Hunting the cymbidium, separating the pricks, cutting even the magnolia, and covering the catkin poplar, it is the new breeze of China, suppressing all weed fragrances. It is the refreshing wind to host the Olympic Games, control the pandemic and create miracles. It's like the air at the edge of Mount Tai, dancing between pines and cypresses, cool and refreshing. It can heal the disease and awaken the ill, brighten eyes, improving hearing capability, and better human body. This is called the mighty wind of the East.

青　玉　案
qīng　　yù　　àn

中　華　風
zhōng　huá　fēng

2021　年　8　月　8　日

和　風　化　雨　潤　萬　物　。
hé　fēng　huà　yǔ　rùn　wàn　wù

悄　悄　進　、　潛　潛　入　。
qiāo　qiāo　jìn　　qián　qián　rù

梅　香　猶　須　風　霜　骨　。
méi　xiāng　yóu　xū　fēng　shuāng　gǔ

韜　光　養　晦　，　勤　勞　苦　心　，
tāo　guāng　yǎng　huì　　qín　láo　kǔ　xīn

一　夜　眾　人　目　。
yī　yè　zhòng　rén　mù

百　煉　更　堅　烈　火　浴　。
bǎi　liàn　gèng　jiān　liè　huǒ　yù

納　長　容　外　陽　關　路　。
nà　cháng　róng　wài　yáng　guān　lù

太　山　松　柏　淩　波　舞　。
tài　shān　sōng　bǎi　líng　bō　wǔ

清　清　涼　涼　，　寧　體　便　人　，
qīng　qīng　liáng　liáng　　níng　tǐ　biàn　rén

風　自　中　華　谷　。
fēng　zì　zhōng　huá　gǔ

14.21　*Sapphire Plate*

The Chinese Breeze

August 8, 2021

Warm wind brings the Spring rain,
Slowly coming in,
Silently percolating,
Moistening soil and nourishing everything.

Plum fragrance comes from winter's prime,
Hide one's strength and bide one's time.
Hardworking and painstaking in fight,
Fame fills the land overnight.

Hardening hundreds of times,
The fire birth is to refine.
Accepting the strengths of others,
The right way to create wonders.

Dancing between mountain trees,
Awakening the ill and healing the disease,
Better human body and brightening eyes,
This is the mighty Chinese breeze.

踏　莎　行
tà　suō　xíng

糊　塗　美　利　堅
hú　tú　měi　lì　jiān

2021 年 11 月 11 日

軟　軟　硬　硬　，
ruǎn　ruǎn　yìng　yìng

真　真　假　假　，
zhēn　zhēn　jiǎ　jiǎ

莽　莽　撞　撞　出　政　策　。
mǎng　mǎng　zhuàng　zhuàng　chū　zhèng　cè

喋　喋　咻　咻　言　中　國　，
dié　dié　xiū　xiū　yán　zhōng　guó

磕　磕　碰　碰　開　錯　車　。
kē　kē　pèng　pèng　kāi　cuò　chē

左　左　右　右　，
zuǒ　zuǒ　yòu　yòu

進　進　出　出　，
jìn　jìn　chū　chū

裏　裏　外　外　盡　楚　歌　。
lǐ　lǐ　wài　wài　jìn　chǔ　gē

上　上　下　下　皆　才　疏　，
shàng　shàng　xià　xià　jiē　cái　shū

糊　糊　塗　塗　看　世　界　。
hú　hú　tú　tú　kàn　shì　jiè

14.22　*Treading the Sedge Path*

Confused America

December 11, 2021

Carrot and stick,

True and fake,

Reckless policies,

Only cause headache.

Chatter and talk,

China always on the block,

Like driving a wrong car,

Bump and ramp in shock.

Left and right stalk,

In and out clog,

All around crises,

No near eleven o'clock.

Top to bottom flock,

Incompetence dock,

Confused America,

The world all mock.

江 月 晃 重 山
jiāng yuè huàng chóng shān

木 秀 中 華
mù xiù zhōng huá

2021 年 11 月 19 日

木 秀 於 林 風 摧 ，
mù xiù yú lín fēng cuī

行 高 於 人 眾 非 。
xíng gāo yú rén zhòng fēi

頂 風 歷 謗 操 不 失 。
dǐng fēng lì bàng cāo bú shī

成 其 名 ，
chéng qí míng

揭 幟 遂 其 誌 。
jiē zhì suí qí zhì

業 精 又 勤 登 頂 ，
yè jīng yòu qín dēng dǐng

行 捷 又 計 造 極 。
xíng jié yòu jì zào jí

高 效 騰 飛 新 模 式 。
gāo xiào téng fēi xīn mó shì

走 其 路 ，
zǒu qí lù

莫 問 所 向 誰 。
mò wèn suǒ xiàng shuí

中美元首虛擬會議有感

14.23   *River Moon Shaking Mountains*

When Better Than the Rest

November 19, 2021

One tree stands out in the forest,
Wind will destroy it to the poorest.
One acts better than all the other,
Public will come up with censure.

Against the wind,
Fighting the slander,
Maintaining the integrity,
Be the persistent leader.

Competence with diligence,
Reaches the peak of excellence.
Action with strategy,
Only comes from prodigy.

A new model of efficiency,
A good rising methodology.
Go your own way,
Do not ask where you will stay.

15 歷　史
li　　shǐ

HISTORY

念 奴 嬌
niàn nú jiāo

鑽 木 取 火
zuàn mù qǔ huǒ

2019 年 11 月 28 日

鑽 木 取 火 ， 文 明 立 ，
zuàn mù qǔ huǒ　wén míng lì

普 羅 米 修 斯 愧 。
pǔ luó mǐ xiū sī kuì

大 禹 治 水 ， 不 拔 誌 ，
dà yǔ zhì shuǐ　bú bá zhì

諾 亞 只 把 水 避 。
nuò yà zhǐ bǎ shuǐ bì

後 羿 射 日 ， 太 陽 神 棄 ，
hòu yì shè rì　tài yáng shén qì

愚 公 把 山 移 。
yú gōng bǎ shān yí

天 地 不 歧 ，
tiān dì bú qí

萬 物 芻 狗 為 祭 。
wàn wù chú gǒu wéi jì

2019 年 11 月 28 日 星期四 美國感恩節

15　歷　史　HISTORY

15.1.1　*Winsome Manner of Maid Niannu*

Drill Wood to Make Fire

November 28, 2019

Drilling wood to make fire,

The civilization starts to transpire.

Prometheus should be ashamed,

Stolen fire can't be acclaimed.

Yu brings the flood under control,

Because of his ambitious soul.

Noah only makes himself a boat,

Avoiding the flood by staying afloat.

Yi chases off nine but one Sun,

Yu Gong moves the mountains blocking his town.

The heaven does not discriminate,

There is no need for things to differentiate.

November 28, 2019, Thursday is America's Thanksgiving Holiday.

15.1.2 念奴嬌
niàn nú jiāo

鈷木取火
zuàn mù qǔ huǒ

2019 年 11 月 28 日

豈能不勞而益？
qǐ néng bú láo ér yì

道天地與人，寰宇四支。
dào tiān dì yǔ rén huán yǔ sì zhī

人居其一，人法地，
rén jū qí yī rén fǎ dì

敬天仍須抗逆。
jìng tiān réng xū kàng nì

民族精神，勤勞誌不移。
mín zú jīng shén qín láo zhì bú yí

我命在己，
wǒ mìng zài jǐ

中華信仰，
zhōng huá xìn yǎng

敬天靠己方逸。
jìng tiān kào jǐ fāng yì

15.1.2　*Winsome Manner of Maid Niannu*

Drill Wood to Make Fire

November 28, 2019

Benefiting without working is not natural,

The four branches of the world are universal.

Law, Heaven, Earth, and People,

Still need to fight besides praying via the steeple.

People is only one of four,

Earth is the land we all adore.

Respect the Earth that grows us all,

Relying on giving will make us fall.

National spirit, Chinese ethos,

It's diligence and perseverance.

My life is mine and I want it to shine,

Chinese faith is to revere heaven and be self-reliant.

豪傑量度
háo jié liàng dù

2020 年 5 月 27 日

胯下大丈夫，
kuà xià dà zhàng fū

兵法謀滿腹，
bīng fǎ móu mǎn fù

如把仁心棄，
rú bǎ rén xīn qì

本亦天下主。
běn yì tiān xià zhǔ

天生霸王福，
tiān shēng bà wáng fú

戰神原貴族，
zhàn shén yuán guì zú

若忍垓下辱，
ruò rěn gāi xià rǔ

他日東山出。
tā rì dōng shān chū

15.2.1　Traits of the Brilliant

May 27, 2020

Enduring the crawling-under-legs insult,

The great man is for the ultimate result.

A master of the art of war,

If not being kind, would have been the emperor.

Natural born the King of the land,

The noble warrior does not aim for the grand.

If only tolerating the one battle shame,

There would be times to reclaim his name.

15.2.2　　　　豪　傑　量　度
　　　　　　　háo　jié　liàng　dù

2020　年　5　月　27　日

加　之　而　不　怒　，
jiā　zhī　ér　bú　nù

臨　之　而　不　怵　，
lín　zhī　ér　bú　chù

仁　智　可　兼　得　，
rén　zhì　kě　jiān　dé

豪　傑　之　量　度　。
háo　jié　zhī　liàng　dù

惜　韓　信　項　羽　，
xī　hán　xìn　xiàng　yǔ

不　慎　在　要　處　，
bú　shèn　zài　yào　chù

僅　因　一　念　差　，
jǐn　yīn　yī　niàn　chā

當　今　世　界　殊　。
dāng　jīn　shì　jiè　shū

15.2.2   Traits of the Brilliant

May 27, 2020

Not getting angry with the wrong blame,
Not afraid when facing the dangerous flame.
With both benevolence and wisdom coexistent,
Display the traits of the brilliant.

Pity Han Xin and Xiang Yu's misfortune,
Unwary at the life's critical junction.
Just because of a wrong thought at a moment,
Today's world would be completely different.

賀　新　郎
hè　xīn　láng

莫　斯　科　不　相　信　眼　淚
mò　sī　kē　bú　xiàng　xìn　yǎn　lèi

2020　年　7　月　1　日

恰　七　十　五　年　，
qià　qī　shí　wǔ　nián

無　蘇　聯　、　二　戰　紀　念　。
wú　sū　lián　　èr　zhàn　jì　niàn

紅　場　改　顏　。
hóng　chǎng　gǎi　yán

不　怪　西　方　奪　話　權　，
bú　guài　xī　fāng　duó　huà　quán

只　因　勝　者　已　換　。
zhī　yīn　shèng　zhě　yǐ　huàn

誌　猶　遠　、　普　京　曾　言　，
zhì　yóu　yuǎn　　pǔ　jīng　céng　yán

強　俄　僅　需　二　十　年　。
qiáng　é　jǐn　xū　èr　shí　nián

四　五　任　、　曙　光　猶　未　現　。
sì　wǔ　rèn　　shǔ　guāng　yóu　wèi　xiàn

巔　峰　時　，　卅　年　前　。
diān　fēng　shí　　sà　nián　qián

15 歷 史 HISTORY

15.3.1 *Congratulating the Groom*

Moscow Does not Believe in Tears

July 1, 2020

Seventy-five years after the World War Two,
Red Square celebration with so much ado.
The once proud Soviet winner non long stood,
The West as sole winner started and grew.

As confident and boasting as Putin knew,
It's election slogan and also his view.
Give twenty years as he said with rue,
I will build Russia strong and anew.

Still ambitious as he likes to pursue,
Four terms and five governments through,
Puzzled Putin found it hard to chew,
Where is the light of glory long overdue?

15.3.2

賀　　新　　郎
hè　　xīn　　láng

莫　斯　科　不　相　信　眼　淚
mò　sī　kē　bú　xiàng　xìn　yǎn　lèi

2020　年　7　月　1　日

記　得　一　夜　閃　電　變　，
jì　dé　yī　yè　shǎn　diàn　biàn

大　帝　國　、　倉　促　試　驗　。
dà　dì　guó　　cāng　cù　shì　yàn

琴　斷　朱　弦　。
qín　duàn　zhū　xián

民　主　資　本　何　競　爭　？
mín　zhǔ　zī　běn　hé　jìng　zhēng

本　不　同　起　跑　線　。
běn　bú　tóng　qǐ　pǎo　xiàn

瞬　息　間　、　一　步　登　天　？
shùn　xī　jiān　　yī　bù　dēng　tiān

沙　皇　青　夢　尋　蹊　徑　，
shā　huáng　qīng　mèng　xún　qī　jìng

要　崛　起　、　惟　憑　蘇　聯　根　。
yào　jué　qǐ　　wéi　píng　sū　lián　gēn

識　真　情　，　不　淚　彈　。
shí　zhēn　qíng　　bú　lèi　tán

15.3.2　*Congratulating the Groom*

Moscow Does not Believe in Tears

July 1, 2020

Once at the world top respecting very few,

Even America was afraid of Khrushchev's shoe.

With Gorbachev's new thought introduced,

A giant social experiment ever ensued.

The whole red empire was like a zoo,

Trying to be others can never be you.

Democracy and free economy may not do,

Racing as a rookie ends only in Timbuktu.

Transcending never suddenly appears,

With innovation the dream could be yours.

Only when seeking the Soviet root of truth,

Can you not believe in Moscow's tears.

七　律
qī　　　lù

不　可　汗　名　留　青　史
bú　kě　wū　míng　liú　qīng　shǐ

2020　年　8　月　15　日

秦　時　夕　照　漢　時　濁　，
qín　shí　xī　zhào　hàn　shí　zhuó

唐　有　中　堂　山　河　破　。
táng　yǒu　zhōng　táng　shān　hé　pò

灰　毀　煙　滅　宋　淚　灑　，
huī　huǐ　yān　miè　sòng　lèi　sǎ

龜　籠　息　鎧　中　華　墮　。
guī　lóng　xī　kǎi　zhōng　huá　duò

人　間　是　非　曲　直　多　，
rén　jiān　shì　fēi　qǔ　zhí　duō

時　代　車　輪　半　遇　挫　。
shí　dài　chē　lún　bàn　yù　cuò

不　可　汗　名　留　青　史　，
bú　kě　wū　míng　liú　qīng　shǐ

敢　問　後　人　不　再　錯　？
gǎn　wèn　hòu　rén　bú　zài　cuò

中國歷史十大罪人：趙(照)高，董卓(濁)，楊國忠(中)，石敬瑭(堂)，宋徽(灰)宗，秦檜(毀)，吳三桂(龜)，乾隆(籠)，慈禧(息)，袁世凱(鎧)。

15.4　*Seven-Character Poem*

Don't Leave a Bad Name in History

August 15, 2020

The Qin dynasty's setting sunshine,

The fall of Han dynasty from the sky.

Broken mountains and rivers in the Tang,

Ashes and tears are always with the Song.

Suffering of modern China starts from Qing,

Only starting now, we see the end is coming.

People with high authority might not know,

Their actions decide where history would go.

The world has many rights and wrongs,

Half is setback where the wheel of times belongs.

Don't leave a bad name in history,

Future leaders make mistakes is not mystery.

綠 背 美 鈔
lù bèi měi chāo

2021 年 2 月 6 日

五 萬 億 量 ， 閘 門 敞 放 ，
wǔ wàn yì liàng zhá mén chǎng fàng

世 界 多 駭 浪 。
shì jiè duō hài làng

看 資 本 市 場 ， 綠 背 美 鈔 ，
kàn zī běn shì chǎng lù bèi měi chāo

十 五 萬 億 ， 值 貶 汪 洋 。
shí wǔ wàn yì zhí biǎn wāng yáng

聯 儲 率 幫 ， 明 奪 暗 搶 。
lián chǔ lù bāng míng duó àn qiǎng

水 漲 股 亦 扛 。
shuǐ zhǎng gǔ yì káng

流 動 性 沖 撞 ，
liú dòng xìng chōng zhuàng

逃 離 現 金 ， 短 策 為 上 。
táo lí xiàn jīn duǎn cè wéi shàng

瘟疫賑災印鈔之感慨。不是投資建議，風險自決自負。

15.5.1 *Slowly Rolled Silk*

Greenbacks

February 6, 2021

Five trillion dollars again,
The gate is way wide open.
The world sees the tsunami,
Scaring both you and me.

Look at the capital markets,
The ever-flooding greenbacks.
Fifteen trillion quantity in total,
An ocean of green bills.

The Federal Reserve,
Leads the dangerous curve,
Rising the money tide,
Robbing people worldwide.

The collision of liquidity,
Pushing up the equity.
Cash is the victim,
Fleeing is the best way to save him.

15.5.2

慢　卷　綢
màn　juàn　chóu

綠　背　美　鈔
lù　bèi　měi　chāo

2021　年　2　月　6　日

歷　史　易　忘　。
lì　shǐ　yì　wàng

宋　交　子　、可　汗　皇　帝　仿　。
sòng　jiāo　zǐ　　kě　hàn　huáng　dì　fǎng

印　錢　把　財　當　，
yìn　qián　bǎ　cái　dāng

交　子　硬　碰　南　墙　，
jiāo　zǐ　yìng　pèng　nán　qiáng

天　下　重　返　銀　兩　。
tiān　xià　chóng　fǎn　yín　liǎng

而　今　蝸　居　，　幾　家　歡　樂　，
ér　jīn　wō　jū　　jǐ　jiā　huān　lè

網　絡　經　濟　長　。
wǎng　luò　jīng　jì　zhǎng

唯　尋　常　巷　陌　，
wéi　xún　cháng　xiàng　mò

百　姓　人　家　，　該　何　收　場　？
bǎi　xìng　rén　jiā　　gāi　hé　shōu　chǎng

15 歷 史 HISTORY

15.5.2 *Slowly Rolled Silk*

Greenbacks

February 6, 2021

History is easy to forget,
The Khan Emperor made big bet.
Printing the money to get rich quick,
It did not do the trick.

The world returned to silver,
Trade got slower.
The invention of Song currency,
Suddenly was all over.

With the pandemic still strong,
Working from home gets long.
Online economy keeps growing,
Wealth gaps become enlarging.

For the average families,
Through the ordinary alleys,
With many people still suffering,
How would all this be ending?

16 看 未 來

kàn　wèi　lái

LOOK INTO FUTURE

鶯　啼　序
yīng　tí　xù

曼　徹　斯　特
màn　chè　sī　tè

2019　年　10　月　5　日

多　見　細　小　車　輛　，
duō　jiàn　xì　xiǎo　chē　liàng

童　話　般　磚　房　。
tóng　huà　bān　zhuān　fáng

昔　昂　昂　、　山　中　教　堂　，
xī　áng　áng　　shān　zhōng　jiāo　táng

今　成　酒　店　長　廊　。
jīn　chéng　jiǔ　diàn　cháng　láng

左　行　道　、　懶　散　兩　旁　，
zuǒ　xíng　dào　　lǎn　sàn　liǎng　páng

象　是　吉　普　賽　女　郎　。
xiàng　shì　jí　pǔ　sài　nǚ　láng

蒸　汽　機　、　幽　暗　廠　房　，
zhēng　qì　jī　　yōu　àn　chǎng　fán

讓　位　商　場　。
ràng　wèi　shāng　chǎng

曼徹斯特：出差兩周是幾年前。

16.1.1　*Prelude of Crowing Warbler*

Manchester

October 5, 2019

Coming from the fairy tales,
The common small vehicles,
And the brick houses,
All in pence and pounds.

Once aloft mountain church,
Now turns into a hotel porch.
The long dark corridor,
More like those in Harry Potter.

Left side driving needs skills,
Roadsides are full of gypsy girls.
Steam engine, factory halls,
Make ways to the shopping malls.

16.1.2　　　　鶯　啼　序
　　　　　　　　yīng　tí　xù

曼　徹　斯　特
màn　chè　sī　tè

2019　年　10　月　5　日

勞　斯　萊　斯　，
láo　sī　lái　sī

偶　見　街　上　，
ǒu　jiàn　jiē　shàng

仍　顯　舊　輝　煌　。
réng　xiǎn　jiù　huī　huáng

不　列　顛　、　寰　球　擴　張　，
bú　liè　diān　　huán　qiú　kuò　zhāng

曾　彎　弓　射　雕　仿　。
céng　wān　gōng　shè　diāo　fǎng

攜　中　原　、　可　汗　掃　蕩　，
xié　zhōng　yuán　　kě　hàn　sǎo　dàng

本　可　暢　、　天　下　別　樣　。
běn　kě　chàng　　tiān　xià　bié　yàng

帶　路　策　，　不　懈　發　揚　，
dài　lù　cè　　bú　xiè　fā　yáng

日　月　重　光　。
rì　yuè　chóng　guāng

帶路策：一帶一路策略，英文是 Belt and Road Initiative，再翻譯成中文就是帶路策。

16.1.2 *Prelude of Crowing Warbler*

Manchester

October 5, 2019

Rolls-Royce car of the elite,

Occasionally seen on the street.

The industrialization story,

Still shows the old glory.

Britain's global expansion,

More like Yuan Dynasty's imitation.

If only Kahn emperor used Han strategy,

The world would be different dramatically.

Current belt and road initiative,

The right path is definitive.

Once there are enough friends,

The sun and the moon will shine again.

16.1.3　　　鶯　啼　序
yīng　tí　xù

曼　徹　斯　特
màn　chè　sī　tè

2019 年 10 月 5 日

閩 人 浙 人 ，
mǐn rén zhè rén

背 井 離 鄉 ，
bèi jǐng lí xiāng

實 五 洲 開 創 。
shí wǔ zhōu kāi chuàng

闖 世 界 、 大 地 為 席 ，
chuǎng shì jiè　dà dì wéi xí

天 空 做 帳 ，
tiān kōng zuò zhàng

四 海 奮 鬥 ，
sì hǎi fèn dòu

知 困 自 強 。
zhī kùn zì qiáng

16.1.3　*Prelude of Crowing Warbler*

Manchester

October 5, 2019

People from Fujian and Zhejiang,
Travel far from one's hometown.
They seem to look for opportunity,
It essentially shows their ingenuity.

Using the earth as the futon,
The sky as the bed-curtain,
Fight globally for a better future,
Through hard time to be stronger.

16.1.4　　　　鶯　　啼　　序
　　　　　　　yīng　　tí　　xù

曼　徹　斯　特
màn　chè　sī　tè

2019　年　10　月　5　日

內　外　開　放　，
nèi　wài　kāi　fàng

你　來　我　往　，
nǐ　lái　wǒ　wǎng

恰　是　登　頂　之　妙　方　。
qià　shì　dēng　dǐng　zhī　miào　fāng

似　殖　民　、　但　更　是　茁　壯　。
sì　zhí　mín　　dàn　gèng　shì　zhuó　zhuàng

秦　人　虎　狼　，
qín　rén　hǔ　láng

九　州　模　式　獨　鰲　，
jiǔ　zhōu　mó　shì　dú　áo

華　夏　寥　廓　高　翔　。
huá　xià　liáo　kuò　gāo　xiáng

16.1.4　*Prelude of Crowing Warbler*

Manchester

October 5, 2019

Opening the country inside and out,
Let people freely go about.
Never let exchange stop,
It's the best way to get to the top.

It's not colonial,
Neither is it imperial.
Qin people of wolf and tiger,
The Chinese model is of desire.

16.1.5　　鶯　啼　序
　　　　yīng　tí　xù

曼　徹　斯　特
màn　chè　sī　tè

2019 年 10 月 5 日

昭　君　文　迪　，
zhāo　jūn　wén　dí

和　親　他　鄉　，
hé　qīn　tā　xiāng

實　為　民　族　望　。
shí　wéi　mín　zú　wàng

日　不　落　、二　牙　曾　嘗　，
rì　bú　luò　　er　yà　céng　cháng

多　少　夢　想　，
duō　shǎo　mèng　xiǎng

付　諸　實　樣　，
fù　zhū　shí　yàng

唯　有　英　邦　。
wéi　yǒu　yīng　bāng

二牙：葡萄牙、西班牙。

16.1.5 *Prelude of Crowing Warbler*

Manchester

October 5, 2019

Zhaojun and Wendi,

Making peace with marriage guarantee.

Heroism of the personal devotion,

The prosperity of the Chinese nation.

The sun would never set,

Portugal and Spain had the taste.

Making it happen from fantasy,

Only Britain put it to reality.

16.1.6

鶯　啼　序
yīng　tí　xù

曼　徹　斯　特
màn　chè　sī　tè

2019　年　10　月　5　日

女　皇　漸　老　，
nǔ　huáng　jiàn　lǎo

川　普　接　棒　，
chuān　pǔ　jiē　bàng

今　盡　露　窮　凶　惡　像　。
jīn　jìn　lù　qióng　xiōng　è　xiàng

滿　世　界　、　忐　忑　心　提　嗓　。
mǎn　shì　jiè　　tǎn　tè　xīn　tí　sǎng

寰　宇　潮　流　浩　蕩　，
huán　yǔ　cháo　liú　hào　dàng

順　之　則　昌　，
shùn　zhī　zé　chāng

逆　之　則　亡　。
nì　zhī　zé　wáng

16.1.6　*Prelude of Crowing Warbler*

Manchester

October 5, 2019

The queen waves from the porch,
Trump takes the torch.
Displaying extremes like a sociopath,
The whole world is taking a deep breath.

The tide of the world is unstoppable,
Going with the flow is plausible.
If you follow, you will prosper,
If you resist, you will suffer.

倫　敦　子　午　線
lún　dūn　zǐ　wǔ　xiàn

2019　年　10　月　19　日

立　足　格　林　威　治　，
lì　zú　gé　lín　wēi　zhì

望　南　北　東　西　。
wàng　nán　běi　dōng　xī

烽　煙　起　、　文　明　爭　執　，
fēng　yān　qǐ　　wén　míng　zhēng　zhí

歷　史　總　在　輪　替　。
lì　shǐ　zǒng　zài　lún　tì

時　易　位　、　陰　陽　規　律　。
shí　yì　wèi　　yīn　yáng　guī　lù

大　趨　勢　不　可　違　避　。
dà　qū　shì　bú　kě　wéi　bì

西　文　明　、　興　盛　至　極　，
xī　wén　míng　　xìng　shèng　zhì　jí

何　能　保　持　？
hé　néng　bǎo　chí

2019 年 10 月 14 日是美國的哥倫布日

16.2.1 *Prelude of Crowing Warbler*

The London Meridian

October 19, 2019

Standing at the zero meridian,

Look at the world as a historian.

Civilization conflicts and wars,

Never stop knocking the doors.

Either to the West or East,

The expansion has never ceased.

Time is always changing,

The cycle of history is repeating.

A thing turns into the opposite,

When pushed to its other limit.

The western civilization reaches the peak,

How can you keep it from getting weak?

16.2.2　鶯啼序
yīng　tí　xù

倫敦子午線
lún　dūn　zǐ　wǔ　xiàn

2019　年　10　月　19　日

歐亞大地，
ōu　yà　dà　dì

豪強疊至，
háo　qiáng　dié　zhì

然青黃不繼。
rán　qīng　huáng　bú　jì

歐列國、大洋征西，
ōu　liè　guó　　dà　yáng　zhēng　xī

盡把印安人欺。
jìn　bǎ　yìn　ān　rén　qī

西班牙、跨洋第一，
xī　bān　yá　　kuà　yáng　dì　yī

葡萄牙、押後跟隨。
pú　táo　yá　　yā　hòu　gēn　suí

昔主人，瑪雅印第，
xī　zhǔ　rén　　mǎ　yǎ　yìn　dì

一絕千裏。
yī　jué　qiān　lǐ

16.2.2 *Prelude of Crowing Warbler*

The London Meridian

October 19, 2019

In the giant land of Eurasia,

Great powers come and disappear.

The granary is nearly empty,

The new crop is not yet ready.

Powerful European countries,

Conquering beyond the boundaries.

Crossing the Atlantic to the West,

How many American Indians are still left?

Transocean Spain is the first,

Portugal comes right the next.

With Maya and Indy no longer in existence,

Rushing torrent flows down to a far distance

16.2.3 鶯　啼　序
yīng　tí　xù

倫　敦　子　午　線
lún　dūn　zǐ　wǔ　xiàn

2019 年 10 月 19 日

人　文　學　家　，
rén　wén　xué　jiā

憑　歷　史　推　，
píng　lì　shǐ　tuī

掌　握　大　趨　勢　。
zhǎng　wò　dà　qū　shì

數　學　家　、　定　義　問　題　，
shù　xué　jiā　　dìng　yì　wèn　tí

數　字　公　式　，
shù　zì　gōng　shì

量　化　形　勢　，
liàng　huà　xíng　shì

把　微　分　積　。
bǎ　wēi　fèn　jī

16.2.3　*Prelude of Crowing Warbler*

The London Meridian

October 19, 2019

Humanities scholars,

Examining the history calendars.

Link all the ends,

To grasp the general trends.

Mathematicians,

More like magicians.

Quantifying all kinds of situations,

Solve problems with formula and equations.

16.2.4　　　鶯　啼　序
　　　　　　　yīng　tí　xù

倫　敦　子　午　線
lún　dūn　zǐ　wǔ　xiàn

2019　年　10　月　19　日

經　濟　學　家　，
jīng　jì　xué　jiā

善　用　統　計　，
shàn　yòng　tǒng　jì

硬　使　混　沌　變　規　律　，
yìng　shǐ　hún　dùn　biàn　guī　lǜ

量　筒　計　、　物　理　最　容　易　。
liàng　tǒng　jì　　wù　lǐ　zuì　róng　yì

西　方　頹　廢　，
xī　fāng　tuí　fèi

活　像　裝　在　量　器　，
huó　xiàng　zhuāng　zài　liàng　qì

明　人　一　看　便　知　。
míng　rén　yī　kàn　biàn　zhī

16.2.4　*Prelude of Crowing Warbler*

The London Meridian

October 19, 2019

Economists,

Make good use of statistics.

Analyzing data to find root causes,

Turn turbulent chaos into laws.

To measure things at an instant,

Physics is the easiest.

West's decline is like being put in a gauge,

People can easily tell even at young age.

16.2.5

鶯　啼　序
yīng　tí　xù

倫　敦　子　午　線
lún　dūn　zǐ　wǔ　xiàn

2019　年　10　月　19　日

潮　流　難　逆　，
cháo　liú　nán　nì

頹　勢　難　避　，
tuí　shì　nán　bì

慌　亂　出　主　意　。
huāng　luàn　chū　zhǔ　yì

一　方　式　、　雖　難　願　意　，
yī　fāng　shì　　suī　nán　yuàn　yì

亦　或　能　成　，
yì　huò　néng　chéng

開　放　邊　境　，
kāi　fàng　biān　jì

放　進　勞　力　。
fàng　jìn　láo　lì

16.2.5 *Prelude of Crowing Warbler*

The London Meridian

October 19, 2019

The tide is hard to reverse,

The decline is only getting worse.

Panic and confusion,

Only create ideas out of illusion.

There is one workable idea,

Even though it may be hard to revere.

Open wide the country's border,

And let in the cheap labor.

16.2.6　　　　鶯　啼　序
　　　　　　　　yīng　　tí　　xù

倫　敦　子　午　線
lún　dūn　zǐ　wǔ　xiàn

2019　年　10　月　19　日

民　主　機　製　，
mín　zhǔ　jī　zhì

依　不　放　棄　，
yī　bú　fàng　qì

只　等　體　量　華　夏　比　。
zhǐ　děng　tǐ　liàng　huá　xià　bǐ

製　造　業　、　該　重　新　回　歸　。
zhì　zào　yè　　gāi　chóng　xīn　huí　guī

只　要　輝　煌　維　繼　，
zhǐ　yào　huī　huáng　wéi　jì

白　人　色　人　，
bái　rén　sè　rén

不　管　比　例　。
bú　guǎn　bǐ　lì

16.2.6　*Prelude of Crowing Warbler*

The London Meridian

October 19, 2019

Democratic institutions,
Still kept without dissolutions.
When it reaches China's magnitude,
All will change the attitude.

Manufacturing suddenly all returns,
There are no more Made in US concerns.
White people, brown people,
If it's okay with things being colorful.

16.3　　　偉　人　時　期　　　　150
　　　　　　　wěi　rén　shí　qī

2020　年　5　月　27　日

世　界　形　勢　诡　異　，
shì　jiè　xíng　shì　guǐ　yì

潮　水　總　是　要　退　。
cháo　shuǐ　zǒng　shì　yào　tuì

不　著　褲　者　終　現　，
bú　zhe　kù　zhě　zhōng　xiàn

偉　人　時　期　將　至　。
wěi　rén　shí　qī　jiāng　zhì

16.3　The Era of the Greats

May 27, 2020

Many peculiar whirls,

Shrouds the current world.

The mighty ocean tide,

Will eventually recede.

Those who don't wear pants,

Will have no more chance.

The times create their heroes,

The era of the Greats narrows.

重樓疊月
chóng　lóu　dié　yuè

新持久戰
xīn　chí　jiǔ　zhàn

2020 年 6 月 4 日

七　八　年　，　國　策　變　，
qī　bā　nián　　guó　cè　biàn

改　革　開　放　啟　，
gǎi　gé　kāi　fàng　qǐ

致　富　路　上　登　。
zhì　fù　lù　shàng　dēng

摸　石　創　新　把　河　過　，
mō　shí　chuàng xīn　bǎ　hé　guò

茫　茫　世　界　不　曾　先　。
máng　máng　shì　jiè　bú　céng　xiān

崇　西　如　日　中　天　，
chóng　xī　rú　rì　zhōng　tiān

八　九　遇　艱　險　，
bā　jiǔ　yù　jiān　xiǎn

幸　得　有　慧　眼　。
xìng　dé　yǒu　huì　yǎn

16.4.1 *Overlapping Towers and Stacking Moons*

New Protracted War

June 4, 2020

In the year of nineteen seventy-eight,
Started a new policy for the Chinese State.
When open reform became a mandate,
China embarked on a road to get rich quick.

Touching stone to cross the uncharted river,
It's an innovation that's unprecedentedly clever.
History rolled forward to nineteen eighty-nine,
The bi-polar world reached its finish line.

Western values were worshipped like divine,
The country went to a stage full of landmine.
Luckily there was not a great Chinese mind,
The world otherwise would need to be redefined

16.4.2

重　樓　疊　月
chóng　lóu　dié　yuè

新　持　久　戰
xīn　chí　jiǔ　zhàn

2020　年　6　月　4　日

戈　氏　心　誌　遭　蒙　騙　，
gē　shì　xīn　zhì　zāo　méng　piàn

一　失　足　成　千　古　恨　，
yī　shī　zú　chéng　qiān　gǔ　hèn

泱　泱　大　國　錚　錚　民　族
yāng　yāng　dà　guó　zhēng　zhēng　mín　zú

仿　西　喪　己　蹶　不　振　！
fǎng　xī　sàng　jǐ　juě　bú　zhèn

央　國　勞　力　有　余　，
yāng　guó　láo　lì　yǒu　yú

西　方　資　本　過　剩　，
xī　fāng　zī　běn　guò　shèng

一　步　一　個　腳　印　，
yī　bù　yī　gè　jiǎo　yìn

全　球　化　各　方　皆　迎　！
quán　qiú　huà　gè　fāng　jiē　yíng

16.4.2　*Overlapping Towers and Stacking Moons*

New Protracted War

June 4, 2020

Gorbachev's single slip of being blind,
Brought a thousand-year sorrow to his land.
A great nation that was not that behind,
Suddenly fell on the world stage sideline.

The Middle Kingdom had abundant people,
The West possessed plentiful of capital.
One step a time reform and open door,
All benefit from globalization sequel.

16.4.3

重 樓 疊 月
chóng lóu dié yuè

新 持 久 戰
xīn chí jiǔ zhàn

2020 年 6 月 4 日

和平演變顏色革命
hé píng yǎn biàn yán sè gé mìng

五眼聯盟更欺壓霸淩，
wǔ yǎn lián méng gèng qī yā bà líng

遍地驕橫！
biàn dì jiāo héng

待到榻邊聞鼾聲，
dài dào tà biān wén hān shēng

方知危機已臨。
fāng zhī wēi jī yǐ lín

遏製再由心頭起，
è zhì zài yóu xīn tóu qǐ

盡顯修昔底德陷阱！
jìn xiǎn xiū xī dǐ dé xiàn jǐng

文明之戰，西方遏製，
wén míng zhī zhàn，xī fāng è zhì

是否能成？
shì fǒu néng chéng

16.4.3　*Overlapping Towers and Stacking Moons*

New Protracted War

June 4, 2020

Subversion through peaceful evolution,
Destabilizing others using color revolution.
Indifferent to other's normal operation,
All is arrogance in every direction.

Until there is a strong competition,
Threatening the insurmountable position.
Containment and cold war segment,
Making everything as an impediment.

The world seems once again,
Falling into the Thucydides entrapment.
The clash of civilizations, the domination,
What would come to us as the final realization?

16.4.4

重　樓　疊　月
chóng　lóu　dié　yuè

新　持　久　戰
xīn　chí　jiǔ　zhàn

2020　年　6　月　4　日

起　初　鄙　視　，
qǐ　chū　bǐ　shì

偶　亦　合　競　，
ǒu　yì　hé　jìng

遏　製　不　停　，
è　zhì　bú　tíng

到　如　今　偏　執　極　端　行　。
dào　rú　jīn　piān　zhí　jí　duān　xíng

紐　約　恐　襲　遇　天　機　，
niǔ　yuē　kǒng　xí　yù　tiān　jī

重　返　亞　洲　卻　換　人　，
chóng　fǎn　yà　zhōu　què　huàn　rén

上　蒼　顧　念　憐　憫　，
shàng　cāng　gù　niàn　lián　mǐn

然　全　面　遏　製　共　識　顯　。
rán　quán　miàn　è　zhì　gòng　shí　xiǎn

16.4.4　*Overlapping Towers and Stacking Moons*

New Protracted War

June 4, 2020

Initially despising,

Occasionally coopetiting.

The containment has never been stopping,

With the paranoid and extreme all now displaying.

New York terror event presented a chance,

The Pivot Asia was a temporary dance.

The ChinAmerica would survive with God's pity,

Until the consensus spiral to create a new enemy.

16.4.5

重　樓　疊　月
chóng　lóu　dié　yuè

新　持　久　戰
xīn　chí　jiǔ　zhàn

2020　年　6　月　4　日

十　裏　埋　伏　，
shí　lǐ　mái　fú

擡　望　眼　中　華　民　族
tái　wàng　yǎn　zhōng　huá　mín　zú

最　危　時　刻　再　面　呈　！
zuì　wēi　shí　kè　zài　miàn　chéng

失　敗　論　讓　地　割　城　，
shī　bài　lùn　ràng　dì　gē　chéng

苟　一　夕　安　寢　。
gǒu　yī　xī　ān　qǐn

焉　知　秦　兵　又　至　，
yān　zhī　qín　bīng　yòu　zhì

虎　狼　環　繞　四　境　，
hǔ　láng　huán　rào　sì　jìng

妥　協　求　和　和　亡　，
tuǒ　xié　qiú　hé　hé　wáng

民　族　復　興　唯　有　抗　爭　！
mín　zú　fù　xìng　wéi　yǒu　kàng　zhēng

16.4.5 *Overlapping Towers and Stacking Moons*

New Protracted War

June 4, 2020

Under ten miles ambush,
The most dangerous push.
The moment of life or death,
Forced upon the Chinese nation in such a rush.

Failure theory more often considered than not,
Belongs to the losing school of thought.
Trade up the land that was hard fought,
Only for one-night of sleep merely bought.

Waking up in the morning facing another day,
Surrounded by the enemy who won't go away.
Compromise for peace and peace will die,
To rejuvenate the nation, we need to fight.

16.4.6

重 樓 疊 月
chóng lóu dié yuè

新 持 久 戰
xīn chí jiǔ zhàn

2020 年 6 月 4 日

速 勝 論 誇 大 西 嫌 ，
sù shèng lùn kuā dà xī xián

帝 國 困 甚 易 妄 言 。
dì guó kùn shèn yì wàng yán

內 團 結 統 一 ，
nèi tuán jié tǒng yī

外 連 接 友 力 ，
wài lián jiē yǒu lì

持 久 抗 衡 就 贏 。
chí jiǔ kàng héng jiù yíng

折 騰 乃 活 力 源 泉 ，
zhē téng nǎi huó lì yuán quán

革 新 才 如 日 方 升 ，
gé xīn cái rú rì fāng shēng

苦 熬 不 亂 終 獲 勝 。
kǔ áo bú luàn zhōng huò shèng

再 過 二 十 年 ，
zài guò èr shí nián

重 登 山 ， 山 頂 。
chóng dēng shān　　shān dǐng

16.4.6 *Overlapping Towers and Stacking Moons*

New Protracted War

June 4, 2020

Quick win theory of the winning kind,
Exaggerating the division of the Western mind.
It's only a denial and a lie,
That superpower is in decline and falling behind.

With strong solidarity and internal unity,
Allying external forces who are friendly.
Hide one's strength and bide one's time,
The protracted war is the winning strategy.

Bold attempts are source of emancipation,
Reform and innovation bring the rejuvenation.
As the morning sun rises from afar,
Slow and Steady will shine like a star.

After twenty years of time,
Hope for the usual mountain climb.
At the pinnacle of the mountain top,
Overlooking a whole new paradigm.

重 樓 疊 月
chóng lóu dié yuè

帝 國 興 衰
dì guó xìng shuāi

2021 年 4 月 24 日

觀 近 代 ， 四 百 載 ，
guān jìn dài   sì bǎi zǎi

阿 姆 斯 特 丹 ，
ā mǔ sī tè dān

首 帝 乃 荷 蘭 。
shǒu dì nǎi hé lán

造 船 征 服 滿 世 界 ，
zào chuán zhēng fú mǎn shì jiè

股 票 始 發 資 本 圈 。
gǔ piào shǐ fā zī běn quān

浩 蕩 搜 括 全 球 ，
hào dàng sōu kuò quán qiú

四 海 把 財 斂 ，
sì hǎi bǎ cái liǎn

鼎 盛 百 余 年 。
dǐng shèng bǎi yú nián

讀債務經濟歷史學家、億萬富翁瑞・達裏奧《變化的世界秩序》有感。

16.5.1　*Overlapping Towers and Stacking Moons*

Rise and Fall of Empires

April 24, 2021

Looking at the modern times,
Four hundred years of history span.
With the world center of Amsterdam,
The first empire was the Netherlands.

With the sails unfurled,
Ships could conquer all over the world.
In the big maritime navigation era,
Ship making brings up great discover.

Stocks were invented for the capital,
The mighty market created the circle.
Attracted money in an innovative way,
Dominating hundred years in its heyday.

16.5.2

重　樓　疊　月
chóng　lóu　dié　yuè

帝　國　興　衰
dì　guó　xìng　shuāi

2021　年　4　月　24　日

濫　用　債　資　不　抵　債　,
làn　yòng　zhài　zī　bú　dǐ　zhài

泛　印　錢　錢　不　值　錢　,
fàn　yìn　qián　qián　bú　zhí　qián

現　代　帝　國　五　洋　馳　騁
xiàn　dài　dì　guó　wǔ　yáng　chí　chěng

一　夜　間　轟　然　塌　陷　。
yī　yè　jiān　hōng　rán　tā　xiàn

後　掀　工　業　革　命　,
hòu　xiān　gōng　yè　gé　mìng

居　上　大　不　列　顛　。
jū　shàng　dà　bú　liè　diān

遍　地　瘋　狂　殖　民　,
biàn　dì　fēng　kuáng　zhí　mín

傲　視　不　夜　地　平　線　。
ào　shì　bú　yè　dì　píng　xiàn

16.5.2 *Overlapping Towers and Stacking Moons*

Rise and Fall of Empires

April 24, 2021

Overuse of capital debt,

Not able to pay back with one's asset.

Over printing of paper money,

Boat load of cash was only worth penny.

The modern empire took on exploration,

Sailing across all the world oceans.

The superpower collapsed overnight,

The cash flooding was too hard to fight.

Then came the industrial revolution,

Great Britain came up with solution.

Colonization was so rampant,

In an empire where the Sun never set.

16.5.3

重 樓 疊 月
chóng lóu dié yuè

帝 國 興 衰
dì guó xìng shuāi

2021 年 4 月 24 日

老 牌 資 本 炮 厲 船 堅
lǎo pái zī běn pào lì chuán jiān

崛 起 衰 敗 前 後 二 百 年 ，
jué qǐ shuāi bài qián hòu èr bǎi nián

遺 跡 猶 見 ！
yí jì yóu jiàn

待 洗 禮 二 次 大 戰 ，
dài xǐ lǐ èr cì dà zhàn

乍 立 阿 美 利 堅 。
zhà lì ā měi lì jiān

只 要 熱 戰 不 本 土 ，
zhī yào rè zhàn bú běn tǔ

管 他 哪 邊 都 無 險 。
guǎn tā nǎ biān dōu wú xiǎn

破 國 爛 城 戰 後 重 建 。
pò guó làn chéng zhàn hòu chóng jiàn

茫 茫 人 寰 ， 千 百 年 間 ，
máng máng rén huán qiān bǎi nián jiān

霸 無 今 悍 。
bà wú jīn hàn

16.5.3　*Overlapping Towers and Stacking Moons*

Rise and Fall of Empires

April 24, 2021

Veteran capitalist's gunboat was strong,
The impact to the world has been long.
Until the World War II was over,
Suddenly stood a giant America.

If the hot war is not on my land,
Either way it will not burn my hand.
The ruined city can be rebuilt after the war,
Not in history seen an empire so powerful.

16.5.4

重　樓　疊　月
chóng　lóu　dié　yuè

帝　國　興　衰
dì　guó　xìng　shuāi

2021　年　4　月　24　日

鬥　轉　星　遷　，
dòu　zhuǎn　xīng　qiān

一　帶　一　路　，
yī　dài　yī　lù

霸　勢　心　展　，
bà　shì　xīn　zhǎn

虎　視　眈　眈　悦　眉　和　顏　。
hǔ　shì　dān　dān　yuè　méi　hé　yán

高　鐵　欲　把　世　界　換　，
gāo　tiě　yù　bǎ　shì　jiè　huàn

昔　日　絲　路　擬　重　綻　，
xī　rì　sī　lù　nǐ　chóng　zhàn

歐　非　渺　遙　萬　裏　，
ōu　fēi　miǎo　yáo　wàn　lǐ

從　此　不　孤　一　衣　相　連　。
cóng　cǐ　bú　gū　yī　yī　xiàng　lián

16.5.4 *Overlapping Towers and Stacking Moons*

Rise and Fall of Empires

April 24, 2021

Things change with the passage of time,
See the world fiercely with pleasant eyes.
Throwing out the Belt Road Initiative,
A brand-new empire is on the climb.

The high-speed rail connects the giant plain,
The old Silk Road is about to bloom again.
Far away to Eurasia, way into Africa,
From then on, China will not be alone.

16.5.5

重　樓　疊　月
chóng　lóu　dié　yuè

帝　國　興　衰
dì　guó　xìng　shuāi

2021　年　4　月　24　日

當　今　霸　主　，
dāng　jīn　bà　zhǔ

見　勢　而　怵　慌　尋　他　途
jiàn　shì　ér　chù　huāng　xún　tā　tú

竟　仿　東　國　基　建　。
jìng　fǎng　dōng　guó　jī　jiàn

照　葫　畫　瓢　無　臉　面　，
zhào　hú　huà　piáo　wú　liǎn　miàn

切　勿　比　己　短　。
qiē　wù　bǐ　jǐ　duǎn

北　從　阿　拉　斯　加　，
běi　cóng　ā　lā　sī　jiā

南　至　阿　根　廷　納　，
nán　zhì　ā　gēn　tíng　nà

統　一　阿　米　麗　卡　，
tǒng　yī　ā　mǐ　lì　kǎ

美　洲　高　鐵　超　級　循　環　。
měi　zhōu　gāo　tiě　chāo　jí　xún　huán

16.5.5　*Overlapping Towers and Stacking Moons*

Rise and Fall of Empires

April 24, 2021

The lone superpower today,
Panicking to find another way.
Imitating the East's infrastructure race,
Not afraid of losing face.

Competing with self's shortcoming,
Never a good idea from the beginning.
Better build a hyperloop America,
From Alaska all the way to Argentina.

16.5.6

重 樓 疊 月
chóng lóu dié yuè

帝 國 興 衰
dì guó xìng shuāi

2021 年 4 月 24 日

人 口 市 場 經 濟 算 ，
rén kǒu shì chǎng jīng jì suàn

規 模 可 把 前 路 斷 。
guī mó kě bǎ qián lù duàn

外 移 民 增 人 ，
wài yí mín zēng rén

內 科 技 再 升 ，
nèi kē jì zài shēng

竟 爭 方 寸 不 亂 。
jìng zhēng fāng cùn bú luàn

脫 鈎 世 界 全 牽 纏 ，
tuō gōu shì jiè quán qiān chán

殺 敵 八 百 己 損 千 ，
shā dí bā bǎi jǐ sǔn qiān

製 度 拼 比 背 水 戰 。
zhì dù pīn bǐ bèi shuǐ zhàn

優 劣 後 人 看 ，
yōu liè hòu rén kàn

竟 天 擇 ， 擇 善 。
jìng tiān zé zé shàn

16.5.6 *Overlapping Towers and Stacking Moons*

Rise and Fall of Empires

April 24, 2021

Population and free market,
The economy is like a space orbit.
Scale can break the road ahead,
If there is no fuel to ascend.

Absorbing immigrants externally,
Foster technology growth internally.
The competition is going on fiercely,
Strategies are executed orderly.

Decoupling is history going back,
The whole world will feel the impact.
Killing eight hundred enemies,
Suffers a thousand self-casualties.

The competition is at ultimate height,
It's a life-or-death fight.
The later generations will see who will win,
The new era is for the winner to begin.

作者簡介

劉月新，江西省新余市人，現居住美國華盛頓州西雅圖。 1984年畢業於江西省新余市一中，同年入北京大學。1988 年畢業於北京大學地球物理系，保送入中國科學院攻讀碩士。1991 年赴美國麻省理工學院留學，師從羅納德・普仁教授。1996 年獲得美國麻省理工學院全球變化科學博士學位並完成麻省理工斯隆商學院工商管理主要課程。曾任美國麻省理工學院中國留學生、學者協會董事，麻省理工學院中國科技協會副總裁。

從事軟件技術開發、實施、企業管理和電商運行管理 25 年。美國微軟公司工作 7 年，任首席高級項目經理，主管微軟在線服務商務平臺運營。歷任芝加哥環球光學公司企業管理系統高級總監，洛杉矶西方電腦公司總架構師。創立了遠信技術公司和環球科技公司。現為環球科技公司總裁。美國項目管理協會成員。曾創新開發了嵌套式軟件设计架構和企業系統爬行程序技術。

愛好哲學、歷史和登山。大學期間，修過厲以寧教授的《西方經濟學》和臺大訪問教授陳鼓應的《先秦哲學》。本科論文研究非線性動力系統和混沌吸引子。

ABOUT THE AUTHOR

Yuexin Liu, born in Xinyu City, Jiangxi Province, China, currently lives in Seattle, Washington State, U.S.A. Yuexin graduated from No. 1 High School of Xinyu City in 1984, went to college in Beijing and graduated with honor and B.S. from the Department of Geophysics of Peking University in 1988. He was admitted to Chinese Academy of Sciences with the Entrance Exam exempted. In 1991, he was admitted to MIT for Ph.D. study under the advice of TEPCO Professor Ronald G. Prinn. Yuexin earned the MIT Ph.D. in Global Change Science and completed majority of the Sloan School MBA program. He served as Board Member of MIT CSSA (Chinese Students and Scholars Association), and VP for MIT CAST (Chinese Association of Science and Technology).

Yuexin has over 25 years of experience in Software Development, Business System Implementation, Business Management and E-Commerce Operations Management. He worked for Microsoft for 7 years, leading the Commerce Platform operations as a Senior Lead Program Manager. He was the Senior Director of ERP (Enterprise Resource Planning) Systems for the Chicago E-Commerce company OpticsPlanet and the Chief Solution Architect for the Los Angeles company Western Computer. Yuexin foundered two companies – Enterprise InfoEdge and Mundus Artis. He is currently the President of Mundus Artis. Yuexin is a member of PMI. He once created the Nested Library software design and crawling technology for Business Systems.

Yuexin is passionate about Philosophy, History and Hiking. During the Baida time, he studied Pre-Qin Philosophers through the class taught by Visiting Professor Guying Chen from Taiwan University. He also studied Western Economics class by Professor Yining Li from Guanghua School. His undergraduate study focused on Non-Linear Dynamic System, Chaos and Attractors.